CATCH!

CATCH!

DANGEROUS TALES *and* MANLY RECIPES *from the* BERING SEA

Travis Lofland

with Chef Jason Lofland

THOMAS NELSON
Since 1798

NASHVILLE   DALLAS   MEXICO CITY   RIO DE JANEIRO

Published in Nashville, Tennessee, by Thomas Nelson. Thomas Nelson is a registered trademark of Thomas Nelson, Inc.

Photography on pages 8, 11, 13, 14, 19, 20, 21, 22, 25, 32, 47, 50, 62, 76, 81, 82, 90, 95, 97, 98, 102, 105, 110, 114, 119, 121, 122, 125, 132, 135, 138, 142, 146, 161, 170, 186, and 206 by Amanda Nicoll Photography

Photography on pages 4, 28, 40, 54, 57, 58, 65, 71, 72, 101, 108, 129, 150, 155, 158, 164, 174, 178, 184, 188, 192, 200, and 203 by Ron Manville with food styling by Teresa Blackburn

Discovery Channel, Deadliest Catch, and related logos are trademarks of Discovery Communications, LLC, used under license. All rights reserved. discovery.com

Thomas Nelson, Inc., titles may be purchased in bulk for educational, business, fund-raising, or sales promotional use. For information, please e-mail SpecialMarkets@ThomasNelson.com.

Library of Congress Cataloging-in-Publication Data

Lofland, Travis, 1973-
 Catch! : dangerous tales and manly recipes from the Bering Sea / Travis Lofland with Jason Lofland.
  p. cm.
 Includes bibliographical references and index.
 ISBN 978-1-4016-0477-6 (alk. paper)
 1. Cooking, American—Pacific Northwest style. 2. Fishing—Bering Sea. 3. Fishing stories. I. Lofland, Jason. II. Title.
 TX715.2.P32L64 2012
 641.5979—dc23

2012000569

Printed in the United States of America

12 13 14 15 16 QGT 6 5 4 3 2 1

CONTENTS

BOAT MEALS FROM THE DEADLY SEAS TO YOUR DECK

"I'LL SHOW YA THE WAY, KID!"

While fishing my first year in southeast Alaska, I met a guy named Matt who worked on the *Aleutian Ballad*. He told me that salmon fishing was sportfishing, and if I wanted a true Alaskan adventure, I should go crabbing in the Bering Sea. So after traveling around Europe all fall, I decided to get a job on a crab boat. So after my cousin randomly runs into a crabbing friend and tells him I'm looking for a job, a phone call and seventy-two hours later, I'm on a Grumman Goose, flying from Dutch Harbor to Akutan to meet the FV seafisher, Capt. Monte Colburn, and the rest of the crew—Mongo, Blinddog, Dave, Cyclops, and John.

What was I thinking as I looked around the boat and met the crew? *I'm going to sea with a group of guys nicknamed Mongo, Blinddog, and Cyclops . . . really?*

One of the first tasks I was given was to chain down the stack. Well, given a quick lesson from the guys on what to do, which translated to me as "Blah, blah, blah" (remember, I'm greener than goose crap), I go to take my second bite on the chain with the chain-binder, pushing with all my might. My arms extend in front of me, instead of putting the cheater bar on my chest and using my body for leverage. Well, the inevitable happens, and I lose my grip and the bar starts flying right at me, about to crush my face. Nope, my crotch caught that cheater bar first. Jockstraps and a cup are not normal crabbing gear. As I'm rolling around on top of the stack, wanting to cry, I hear laughing from the wheelhouse ('cause, of course, I'm all the way back right in front of the wheelhouse). I roll over from my fetal position and look up, and here's Mongo, my deck boss, laughing hysterically, then saying, "You're doing it all wrong, Horn." I'm thinking to myself, *No kidding!* as he tells me, "I'll show ya tha way, kid. Didn't those other guys help ya?"

At this point I figure it'd be best to listen to everything this eight-fingered man has to say! We left town that night, and the next five weeks my life was just a blur. It was halfway through my first trip when my hands turned into clubs. I was sittin' in the galley, eating breakfast, when Captain Monte comes in and sees me trying to hold a fork to eat waffles and dropping it consecutive times onto my plate. He looked at me and said, "Oh, kid, you got it bad."

"What *is* that?" I asked.

"The claw," he said.

"Well, is it going to get any better?" I asked, and he replied, "It's going to get a lot worse before its gets any better."

And he was right. As a greenhorn, your body isn't used to the grueling punishment of crabbing. And you do one of two things: suck it up or quit! Since *quit* has never been in my vocabulary, you just drive on, which was instilled in me through the army. So drive on I did.

Everybody had their own way of training you. There were the guys who would watch you flounder. There was Blinddog, who told me how stupid and worthless I was; and Mongo, who kept telling me, "Stick with it, kid, I'll show you the way."

Finally, one day, I hit a groove while setting gear. When we were heading in the house, Mongo patted me on the shoulder and said, "You keep that up, kid. You're getting there."

It was a few days later when Cyclops was pinned under a pot while setting gear. He got lucky. The other stack man was on the stack, and broke the #1 rule of working above the rest of the crew and unsecured a pot without hooking it up to the crane first. On the next roll of the boat he found himself riding the pot off of the stack like a bull rider onto a pot in the launcher, pinning Cyclops to the deck, banging him up but not killing him, leaving us to finish our first trip a man down.

We made our first delivery in the Pribilofs on the island of St. Paul to a floater processer and made a touch-and-go to get new personnel. Terry, a.k.a. Cyclops, was going home. So here comes our new engineer, Doug, a man who had half an arm but was a magician in the engine room.

Our second trip was much of the same, always under the watchful eye of my deck boss, Mongo, who always let me struggle doing things my way before showing me the easy way . . .

Cornflake-Crusted Creamy
Mushroom Pork Chops

Butt-Kickin' Braised Spareribs

On-the-Boat Beer Can Chicken

High Seas Stroganoff

Seafaring Shepherd's Pie

Crabby Patty's Chicken Pot Pie

Burrito in a Cup

Superstitious Stormbird Turkey

I Wish This Was More Than
a Cheese Sandwich

Nuked King Crab Legs

In a Pinch Potatoes

Mariner's Meatloaf

Chillin' Chile con Carne

No Time for Meatballs Spaghetti

Anchored Accidental
Shrimp Skewers

Travis Taters

Sailor's Stuffed Bell Peppers

CORNFLAKE-CRUSTED CREAMY MUSHROOM PORK CHOPS

This recipe is a collaboration of two recipes in one. I woke up from my sleep shift and one of the other deckhands was cooking pork chops coated in cornflakes, so I decided to add that technique to my favorite way to prepare pork chops, which is with cream of mushroom soup.

1 Preheat the oven to 350°F.

2 Place a large saucepan over medium heat and add enough oil to coat the bottom of the pan.

3 Salt and pepper the flour to taste, and coat pork chops generously with flour. Dip pork chops in egg and then roll them in cornflake crumbs. Cook over medium heat in oil until golden brown.

4 Place cooked pork chops in a full-size (20 x 12-inch) hotel pan or disposable foil pan and cover with the soup. Sprinkle with the minced garlic. Cover with tinfoil and bake for 2 hours.

Makes 25 to 30 servings

oil for frying

salt and pepper, for seasoning

2 cups flour

25 to 30 pork chops

10 eggs, whisked

1 box cornflakes, crushed into crumbs

2 (64-ounce) cans cream of mushroom soup

2 tablespoons minced garlic

BRO' NOTE:

MAKE SURE TO SEASON YOUR FLOUR WITH SALT AND PEPPER BEFORE BREADING THE PORK.

Everyone loves rib night on the boat. Since we don't have a grill, these ribs are slowly braised in the oven. You have to do what you have to do when miles from shore.

BUTT-KICKIN' BRAISED SPARERIBS

1 Preheat the oven to 300°F.

2 To make the rub, in a large mixing bowl combine the paprika, granulated garlic, onion powder, dry mustard, cumin, brown sugar, celery salt, sugar, cayenne, white, and black peppers, and iodized salt, and mix well.

3 Season the ribs with the rub, coating generously.

4 Place the ribs in a large baking pan with 1¼ cups water. Bake, covered, for 2 to 3 hours or until shrunk up the bone ½ inch. Let rest and serve.

Serves 15 hungry sailors

BRO' NOTE:

To take it one step further and acquire a smoky flavor, add 2 tablespoons of liquid smoke to the braising liquid.

½ cup paprika

2 tablespoons granulated garlic

2 tablespoons onion powder

2 tablespoons dry mustard

2 tablespoons cumin

2 tablespoons brown sugar

2 tablespoons celery salt

1 tablespoon sugar

2 tablespoons cayenne pepper

2 tablespoons white pepper

2 tablespoons black pepper

1 tablespoon iodized salt

6 racks spareribs

1¼ cups water

ON-THE-BOAT BEER CAN CHICKEN

¼ cup paprika

1 tablespoon granulated garlic

1 tablespoon onion powder

1 tablespoon dry mustard

1 tablespoon cumin

1 tablespoon brown sugar

1 tablespoon celery salt

½ tablespoon sugar

1 tablespoon cayenne pepper

1 tablespoon white pepper

1 tablespoon black pepper

½ tablespoon iodized salt

2 whole chickens

2 cans beer

8 to 12 softball-size tinfoil balls

So, the first time I did Beer Can Chicken on the boat was quite the learning experience. As you can imagine, the Bering Sea is constantly changing, and this day was no different. I put the birds in the stove with the normal precautions and care; went back out on deck in flat, calm weather; and started hauling gear again.

Over the next couple of hours, the tide turned around and the seas picked up a little, nothing savage, but enough to get the birds to tip over in the pan, splashing olive oil and chicken drippings onto the hot oven floor and filling the entire house with an eye-watering, rancid smoke. It was quite disheartening when the captain said over the loud-hailer, "Hey, Trav, I think dinner is going nuclear."

I ran into the galley and started coughing as I opened the oven and saw dinner tipped over. Fortunately, the dinner was saved and was a hit, but on the flip side, the house reeked for a couple of days. So I went back to the drawing board and came up with some ideas to keep the birds from tipping over: note the tinfoil balls.

1 To make the rub, in a large mixing bowl, combine the paprika, granulated garlic, onion powder, dry mustard, cumin, brown sugar, celery salt, sugar, cayenne, white, and black peppers, and iodized salt.

2 Rub the chickens with the dry rub and let stand in the fridge overnight, if possible. Reerve 2 tablespoons of the rub for later.

3 When ready to prepare, preheat the oven to 300°F.

4 Open the beer cans and drink two gulps out of each beer, or pour out a couple of slurps if you're at work. Place 1 tablespoon of rub in each beer. Gently insert a beer into the cavity of each chicken. Stand chickens up in a roasting pan and place tinfoil balls around the chickens in case of big seas. Bake for 2 hours.

Makes 8 to 10 servings

BRO' NOTE:

BE GENTLE WHEN INSERTING THE
BEER CANS, 'CAUSE CHICKENS HAVE
FEELINGS TOO.

HIGH SEAS STROGANOFF

This High Seas Stroganoff is actually an oxymoron because boiling pots in high seas can turn into a mess, or worse, burn blisters and require a trip to the burn unit.

3 (.87-ounce) packets of au jus mix (to make 9 cups)

1 institutional-sized (60-ounce) can mushrooms

2 tablespoons minced garlic

4 pounds beef or tri-tip leftovers

2 tablespoons cornstarch

2 (16-ounce) packages egg noodles

1 (16-ounce) container sour cream

1 Make the au jus mix according to package directions. Add the 'shrooms, garlic, and meat leftovers to the au jus. Bring to a boil and let simmer for 30 minutes. Thicken with cornstarch and reduce the heat to low.

2 Meanwhile, cook the noodles according to the package directions and drain.

3 To serve, stir the sour cream and then the noodles into the thickened stroganoff.

Makes 10 to 15 servings

BRO' NOTE:

THIS IS A SIMPLIFIED VERSION FOR AT SEA, BUT IF YOU WANT TO ADD A DIFFERENT KICK, ADD SLICED DILL PICKLES TO THE MIX.

This is a dish that my mom used to make, and to make it seaworthy I added garlic powder and cheese to the mashed potatoes.

1 Preheat the oven to 350°F.

2 In a large bowl, prepare the instant mashed potatoes according to the package directions. Add the Parmesan cheese and minced garlic. Set aside.

3 In a Dutch oven or oven-safe pan with a lid, brown the ground beef. Drain the fat and discard. Add the veggies and soup. Season with the granulated garlic. Bring to a boil, then remove from the heat.

4 Top with the Cheddar cheese and then with the mashed potatoes. Bake in the oven for one hour or until potatoes are golden brown.

Makes 10 to 15 servings

SEAFARING SHEPHERD'S PIE

1 (16-ounce) box instant mashed potato mix

1/2 cup Parmesan cheese

2 tablespoons minced garlic

5 pounds ground beef

1 onion, chopped

2 1/2 pounds frozen peas and carrots

2 (14- to 16-ounce) cans corn, drained

2 (16-ounce) cans green beans, drained

3 cans tomato soup

1 tablespoon granulated garlic

Cheddar cheese, for melting on top

BRO' NOTE:

TO MAKE THE PRESENTATION A LITTLE FANCIER, USE A PIPING BAG FOR THE INSTANT TATERS ON THE TOP.

CRABBY PATTY'S CHICKEN POT PIE

4½ cups Bisquick baking mix

2 eggs

1 cup milk

1 cup shredded Cheddar cheese

vegetable oil, for frying

5 pounds chicken breasts, cubed

1 onion, diced

2 tablespoons minced garlic

1 teaspoon crushed red pepper

8 ounces Normandy blend frozen vegetables

4 cups water

4 packets McCormick chicken gravy mix

I won't lie. This is the recipe off the back of a Bisquick box. I add eggs and cheese for fluff and texture. This never lasts long in the galley, and there are never leftovers.

1 Preheat the oven to 450°F.

2 In a large bowl mix the Bisquick, eggs, milk, and cheese. Set aside.

3 In a large saucepan over medium-high heat, pour in the vegetable oil and brown the chicken. Drain the excess oil from the pan. Add the onions, garlic, pepper, and frozen veggie mix. Sauté with the chicken until the vegetables are cooked through. Add 4 cups of water and the chicken gravy packets. Bring to a boil and simmer until thickened.

4 Place the chicken and vegetable mixture in a 13- x 9-inch baking pan. Top with the Bisquick mix and bake for 20 to 30 minutes.

Makes 10 to 15 servings

BRO' NOTE:

WHICH GIRLFRIEND IS CRABBY PATTY? I DON'T THINK I HAVE MET HER YET.

This recipe came from Doug Stanley, a producer from the show and a former river guide in the Grand Canyon. He was telling me how he used to layer all the fixin's for a burrito in paper cups so he wouldn't have to deal with a tortilla with gloved hands . . . I tried it, and he was right.

BURRITO IN A CUP

1 In each of six paper cups, start with a layer of black beans.

2 Next layer with meat, cheese, and salsa.

3 Top with sour cream and a little more cheese for garnish.

Makes 6 servings

2 (15.5-ounce) cans of black beans

leftover taco meat

shredded cheese

salsa

sour cream

SUPERSTITIOUS STORMBIRD TURKEY

This is a great comfort food, but on a boat it is considered bad luck to cook a turkey. A lot can happen in four to six hours on a boat in the icy-cold waters of the Bering Sea, but if you can pull it off, you will be eating good for a day or two on this bird.

1 (20-pound) turkey

2 cups (4 sticks) butter, softened

¼ cup kosher salt

2 tablespoons garlic salt

2 tablespoons ground pepper

1 onion, quartered

1 Preheat the oven to 325°F.

2 Rub the turkey all over with butter, salt, garlic salt, and pepper, and place in a foil roasting pan. Place the onions in the bottom of the pan, around the turkey, and cover with foil. Bake for 4 to 6 hours or until the internal temperature reaches 155°F. Remove foil during the last hour, if possible, to brown.

Makes 10 to 15 servings

I WISH THIS WAS MORE THAN A CHEESE SANDWICH

This is something we make and eat when there is no time for a break but we need something in our stomachs.

1 Spread the mayo on both pieces of bread. Add the cheese. Put it all together, and bon appétit.

Makes 1 serving

mayonnaise, for spread

2 slices bread

2 slices Kraft Singles

BRO' NOTE:

First sandwich I ever made as a kid. Some people use Miracle Whip for added tang.

Given the rare opportunity of being on the deck of a crab boat while fishing for king crab, you occasionally come across an injured crab who is missing a leg. In this instance you throw back the crab, but if you happen to find the missing leg, you will be eating well at break time. This is a quick fix that will put a smile on your face and a stop to the growling stomach.

NUKED KING CRAB LEGS

1 Place the leg in the microwave and cook for 40 seconds. Flip the crab leg.

2 Put the butter in a bowl and place it in the microwave with the leg. Cook for another 40 seconds, eat—and get back to work.

1 fresh king crab leg
4 tablespoons butter

Makes 1 serving

BRO' NOTE:

NORMALLY, I WOULD NEVER MICROWAVE A KING CRAB LEG—EVER—BUT AFTER A 20-HOUR WORKDAY IN THE BERING SEA, THIS IS PROBABLY THE BEST CRAB EVER.

IN A PINCH POTATOES

The perfect baked potato is cooked in the oven with a metal skewer. While at sea, though, you don't have all the amenities of your household kitchen, so you have to improvise. I used metal butter knives, which did the trick in a pinch. The potatoes turned out just how I like them. Crispy, thick skin and soft in the middle.

6 large potatoes

1 Preheat the oven to 350°F.

2 Wash the potatoes, and insert a knife lengthwise into each potato. Bake for 1 to 1½ hours until the outsides are crisp and the insides are soft. Top with your favorite baked potato toppings.

Makes 6 servings

BRO' NOTE:

THIS IS A TRUE "BAKED" POTATO BECAUSE IF YOU COOK THEM IN FOIL, YOU ARE ACTUALLY STEAMING THE POTATO.

1 Preheat the oven to 350°F.

2 In a large bowl, combine the ground beef, eggs, onion, bell pepper, garlic, breadcrumbs, tomato, coffee grounds, smoked paprika, salt, pepper, Worcestershire sauce, jalepeño, and tomato paste and mix well. Form into a loaf and place on a large sheet pan. Wrap the bacon slices around the loaf at an angle. Bake for 1 hour. Remove from the oven and let the loaf rest for 10 minutes. Slice and serve with mashed potatoes and canned corn.

Makes 15 servings

MARINER'S MEATLOAF

5 pounds ground beef

4 eggs

1 onion, chopped

1 bell pepper, chopped

4 cloves garlic, minced

1 cup breadcrumbs

1 tomato, diced

1 tablespoon coffee grounds (not instant)

1 tablespoon smoked paprika

2 tablespoons salt

2 tablespoons pepper

1 tablespoon Worcestershire sauce

1 jalepeño, diced

1 can tomato paste

6 slices bacon

CHILLIN' CHILE CON CARNE

1 Preheat a large saucepan over medium-high heat. Add the ground beef and brown. Add the onions, garlic, celery, peppers, and green chiles. Cook for 3 to 4 minutes. Stir in the chili powder, cumin, garlic powder, and coriander. Add the tomatoes, tomato paste, and beer and bring to a boil. Let simmer for 1 hour. Salt and pepper to taste.

2 Serve with cornbread or tortilla chips. Top with sharp Cheddar cheese.

Makes 20 servings

5 pounds ground beef

1 large onion, chopped

4 cloves garlic, minced

4 stalks celery, chopped

2 bell peppers, chopped

1 jalapeño, diced

1 (32-ounce) can chopped green chiles

1/4 cup chili powder

2 tablespoons cumin

2 tablespoons garlic powder

1 tablespoon coriander

1 (#10) can diced tomatoes

1 small can tomato paste

1 bottle dark beer

salt and pepper, to taste

sharp Cheddar cheese, grated

NO TIME FOR MEATBALLS SPAGHETTI

While working in the Bering Sea, time for prepping food is hard to come by, and one of my favorite comfort foods is spaghetti and meatballs. But making meatballs is time-consuming, so to save time I use bratwurst. This is a great substitute for meatballs, with the unique flavor of the bratwurst, that goes great with marinara sauce.

1 Heat a large saucepan over medium heat. Add 2 tablespoons of the olive oil and brown the bratwurst in the oil, cooking until all sides are golden brown. Add the onion, garlic, and pepper, and cook for 1 to 2 minutes.

2 Reduce the heat to low, add the sauce and Italian seasoning, and simmer for 1 hour.

3 Fill a large stockpot with water and bring to a boil. (For two pounds of pasta, you are gonna want to use 1 gallon of water. Remember to add plenty of salt to the water.) Cook the spaghetti for 10 to 12 minutes or as directed on the box. Strain and toss with the remaining 1 tablespoon of olive oil to prevent the pasta from sticking together. Plate and serve with the sauce, garlic bread, and grated Parmesan cheese.

Makes 15 servings

3 tablespoons olive oil, divided

2 packages Johnsonville bratwurst, cut into 1-inch rounds

1 onion, small dice

2 garlic cloves, minced

1 bell pepper, small dice

2 (32-ounce) jars of your favorite spaghetti sauce

2 tablespoons Italian seasoning

1 (32-ounce) package spaghetti

BRO' NOTE:
If you don't want the meatball look, you can remove the skin from the bratwurst and it will be more like a bolognese or meat sauce.

ANCHORED ACCIDENTAL SHRIMP SKEWERS

2 pounds fresh shrimp

1 bottle Italian salad dressing

It was one of those salmon-fishing summers where we hadn't made a dime, and we were waiting on the fish to show up. We had been in Valdez for two and a half weeks and not so much as a fish caught. It was cheaper to sit in Anderson Bay and camp out than stay tied to the docks with the opportunity to spend what little cash we had up at the bar when our boat was stocked for three months of fishing. We had a grill, charcoal, steaks, a vacuum sealer, fishing poles, lures, skiffs, and guns. We were pretty much set up to have one heck of a camping trip.

We also had our shrimp pots, and we were eating fresh shrimp every possible way. I hate to use a line from *Forrest Gump*, but for real, we had eaten boiled shrimp, fried shrimp, shrimp gumbo, shrimp creole . . . You get the idea.

We'd decided to do some steaks and mix it up and put a different taste in our months, and last minute decided to throw a couple skewered shrimp on the barbie. I just grabbed some Italian salad dressing, marinated the shrimp for about fifteen minutes, skewered 'em, and grilled 'em. They were phenomenal.

The dressing will flame up a bit, but that sears the flavor in. Make sure not to overcook. Seafood is always best prepared medium. After all, they are already dead.

1 Pull the heads off, peel, and devein the shrimp. Marinate in Italian dressing for an hour.

2 If using wooden skewers, soak them in water 20 minutes before you're ready to skewer the kabobs.

3 Preheat the grill. Skewer the shrimp and grill for about 2 to 3 minutes per side until shrimp are medium, considering these babies just came out of the water.

Makes 8 to 10 servings

TRAVIS TATERS

The first time I made these, I was dreaming of a loaded baked potato while pulling gear, and when dinner came around, I made this work on the fly. Definitely satisfies the craving after coming in from the wet and cold deck of the crab boat.

1 (32-ounce) box instant mashed potatoes

1 cup shredded pepper jack cheese

½ cup sour cream

½ cup bacon bits

1 Prepare the potatoes according to the directions on the box. Stir in the shredded cheese, sour cream, and bacon bits and serve.

Makes 8 to 10 servings

BRO' NOTE:

THIS SOUNDS LIKE A GOOD SIDE FOR THE SUPERSTITIOUS STORMBIRD TURKEY (PAGE 18). I WANT TO KNOW WHAT HAPPENS WHEN YOU DREAM OF POTATO SALAD.

1 Preheat the oven to 350°F.

2 Cut the tops off the peppers and remove the seeds. Set aside.

3 In a large bowl, mix the ground beef, egg, onion, rice, breadcrumbs, Worcestershire, and salt and pepper.

4 Stuff each pepper with the meat mixture.

5 Wrap each pepper in tinfoil and place on a baking sheet. Bake for 1½ hours.

Makes 2 servings

2 large green bell peppers, washed

1½ pounds ground beef

1 egg

1 tablespoon diced onion

1 tablespoon uncooked rice

½ cup dried breadcrumbs

½ teaspoon Worcestershire sauce

salt and pepper, to taste

EXCURSION ENTREES: UNCONVENTIONAL MEALS FOR ON-THE-GO ADVENTURES

FIRST RACE

My first time in a race boat was a little less than perfect, but nothing short of an outstanding experience.

Captain Monte was the first to go out and make a lap. He climbed out of the boat with a big smile, hollerin', "That was more fun than Disneyland."

And then it was my turn to get strapped in—oxygen tank strapped on and full F-16 mask—and I was ready to go.

I was hangin' on every word the throttle man, Mark Kawoulski, had to say while idling out, and the next thing I know we're flying across the water of Sarasota Bay at 110 miles per hour, all while Mark is coaching me how to handle the corners. Next thing you know, he's cut power and sets me down and I start turning at 90 miles an hour and accelerating coming out to 120 miles per hour down the next straightaway, and he's asking if I want to do another lap.

"Do you think I'm stupid? Of course I want to do another lap."

This time he tells me to roll in a little harder, and when I feel her start to drift, I roll out and he'll really give her the coals.

We sat the boat down and rolled into the corner at over 100 miles per hour this time, just flyin', rolled in, started to loosen up, and rolled out, and

we were off to 130 miles per hour, this time down the bay, with Jet Skis and sailboats just a blur as we rocket across the bay.

I think it was the moment when Mark said I did good for a first-timer that I decided to become a powerboat racer. It only took another two years, a lot of persistence, and the right phone calls to get it all started. My good buddy Scotty Begovich from the Miss Geico offshore racing team finally got the ball rolling after several e-mails and phone calls.

I'll never forget my first conversation with my race partner, Bob Mazikowski—a Georgia boy whose neck is as red as Alabama clay. I could tell this guy was passionate about racing when he told me that if you want to be an offshore racer, you've got to be willing to grab ten thousand dollars cash, walk out to the end of the dock with five of your best friends, each of them with a sack of potatoes, throw the money in the wind, let your buddies beat ya with the spuds, and if you pick yourself up and do it again the next week, you just might be an offshore racer.

Well, I flew down to Atlanta to meet Bob and go for a boat ride. That did nothing but seal the deal . . . in my second race boat—not as big and fast as the first, but an even wilder ride.

Trish the Dish Peanut Butter,
Mayo, and Banana Sandwich

Beef Tornados

Gone-Fishing Goulash

Backyard Pork Burrito

Jamaican Jerk Beef Kabobs

Shipwreck Ceviche

Finger-Lickin' Chicken

At Sea Sashimi

24-Egg Campfire Omelet

Firecrackin' Shrimp Brochette with
Jalapeños and Pepper Jack

Campfire Fish Sticks

Waimanu Valley Herbed Butter Scampi

Spam and Egg Breakfast Sandwich

Poor Man's Lobster

This delicious, on-the-go recipe hails from my beautiful friend and former deck boss, Trisha. We were fishing for salmon on her father's fifty-eight-foot Delta fishing boat, the *Desert Storm*.

We had just made a set, and Trish came out of the house with what looked like a normal peanut-butter-and-something sandwich and offered me a bite. "Sure," I replied and took a big ol' bite. It was the creamiest peanut butter sandwich, with something I couldn't quite put a finger on. Then I noticed the smirk on Trish's face. I asked her what I was eating, and she told me it was a peanut butter mayo sandwich. I almost lost it—and then realized it was pretty good.

She then turned, laughing, and grabbed her own sandwich out of the galley. "I made two, thinking you would want one too."

TRISH THE DISH PEANUT BUTTER, MAYO, AND BANANA SANDWICH

peanut butter

2 slices bread

mayonnaise

1 banana, sliced

1 Spread peanut butter on one slice of bread and mayo on the other slice. Place the bananas on top of the peanut butter and put the bread together to form your sandwich.

Makes 1 serving

BRO' NOTE:

SOUNDS LIKE THE ONLY THING YOU'RE MISSING IS A PICKLE.

BEEF TORNADOS

2 pounds baron of beef

Salt and pepper, to taste

Johnny's Seasoning Salt

6 slices bacon

1/4 cup Italian
salad dressing

1 Cut baron of beef into 1/4-inch-thick strips, 18 inches long. Season the strips with salt, pepper, and seasoning salt. Roll each strip with a slice of bacon and secure with wooden skewers. Marinade in Italian dressing for 1 hour.

2 If using wooden skewers, soak them in water 20 minutes before you're ready to skewer the kabobs.

3 Preheat the grill and add the skewers. Grill 6 to 8 minutes for medium. Remove from the grill and allow to rest 5 minutes before serving.

Makes 4 servings

Goulash is a family recipe of my mother's, and if we were out fishing and did not catch, we could easily heat up some goulash and be happy.

1 Fry the bacon in a medium frying pan over medium heat until crispy. Remove from the pan, leaving the drippings in the pan, and drain the bacon on paper towels.

2 In the remaining bacon fat, fry the ground beef, onions, and celery until the onions are translucent. Drain and set aside.

3 Bring a large stockpot of water to boil over high heat. Salt the water generously, add the pasta, and boil for 10 minutes or until almost tender. Drain. Combine the hamburger mixture with the pasta. Add the tomatoes, tomato sauce, and ketchup. Salt and pepper to taste, cover, and simmer over low heat for 1 hour. Stir in the fried bacon. Serve with bread and butter.

Makes 10 to 12 servings

GONE-FISHING GOULASH

1 pound bacon, diced

1½ pounds ground beef

1 onion, diced

½ celery stalk, diced

5 cups macaroni

2 (32-ounce) cans stewed tomatoes

1 (16-ounce) can tomato sauce

½ cup ketchup

salt and pepper to taste

BRO' NOTE:

PASTA COOKED ALMOST TENDER IS CALLED AL DENTE. IN THIS DISH THE PASTA WILL FINISH COOKING IN THE PAN WITH THE REST OF THE INGREDIENTS, ABSORBING THE FLAVOR OF THE GOULASH.

BACKYARD PORK BURRITO

1 boneless pork butt

1/4 cup cumin

1/4 cup coriander

1/4 cup kosher salt

2 tablespoons black pepper

2 Anaheim peppers

Flour tortillas

1 (7-ounce) can salsa verde

1 (16-ounce) can refried beans

1 cup shredded Cheddar cheese

1 jar of your favorite salsa

Well, this is my simplified version of chile verde that you wrap in a burrito that is cooked in or on a campfire. Once the pork is in a wrap, you really don't even need a plate. Just fold, roll, and eat.

1 Rub the pork butt with the cumin, coriander, salt, and pepper, and let it sit in the fridge overnight.

2 In the morning, before your camping trip, you are gonna want to sear all sides of the pork butt in a cast-iron skillet.

3 Once seared, wrap the pork in foil and place on ice in a cooler.

4 Once your camp is set up and your fire has burnt down where you have some coals, wrap the pork in foil one more time, and place the wrapped pork butt in the fire and surround with coals.

5 Let the pork cook for 4 to 5 hours, rotating and flipping every hour or so.

6 Halfway through the roasting time, roast your peppers on the fire, on a grill, until the outsides of the peppers are black and charred. Place the roasted peppers in a plastic bag, seal, and let them steam in the bag.

7 After 4 or 5 hours, the pork will have shrunk in the foil and will be kind of soft in there. This is how you know it is done. Remove from the fire and let it rest for 15 minutes.

8 Meanwhile, wrap the tortillas in foil and place them on the grill, flipping often so they don't burn.

9 Dice the peppers and set aside.

10 Remove the foil from the pork and shred it into a pot. Add the salsa verde and diced Anaheim peppers.

11 In a separate pot, heat your beans.

12 Remove the tortillas from the fire and layer with beans, pork, cheese, and salsa. Fold and serve. My son says that this is the best camping food ever.

Makes 8 to 10 burritos

BRO' NOTE:

TRAVIS: THIS IS A RECIPE I AM GONNA HAVE TO TRY ON THE BOYS.

JAMAICAN JERK BEEF KABOBS

1 In a zip-top bag combine the green onions, allspice, red wine vinegar, salt, thyme, soy sauce, cinnamon, nutmeg, habaneros, sirloin, bell pepper, and plantains. Place in the refrigerator and marinate for 2 to 4 hours.

2 If using wooden skewers, soak them in water 20 minutes before you're ready to skewer the kabobs.

3 Pour off the liquid and skewer the sirloin, peppers, and plantains.

4 Preheat the grill over medium heat.

5 Grill the kabobs for about 3 minutes per side for medium-rare.

Makes 6 to 8 servings

1/2 cup chopped
green onion

1 tablespoon allspice

2 tablespoons red
wine vinegar

1 teaspoon salt

1 teaspoon thyme

2 teaspoons soy sauce

1/2 teaspoon cinnamon

1/4 teaspoon nutmeg

2 habanero peppers

1 1/2 pounds beef sirloin,
cut into chunks

1 red bell pepper,
cut into chunks

2 plantains, sliced
into chunks

SHIPWRECK CEVICHE

1 pound (21–25) shrimp

1/2 cup lime juice, divided

1 jalapeño, diced

1/2 cup chopped cilantro

1/2 sweet onion, thinly sliced

1 cucumber, deseeded and diced

salt and pepper to taste

1 Peel and devein the shrimp and place in a large bowl. Add 1/4 cup of the lime juice and soak overnight. The acid from the lime juice will cook the shrimp.

2 In the morning drain off the lime juice. Add the remaining 1/4 cup of lime juice, the jalapeño, cilantro, onion, and cucumber to the bowl. Let stand for 3 to 4 hours. Taste for salt and pepper. Serve with tortilla chips.

Makes 8 servings

FINGER-LICKIN' CHICKEN

Finger-Lickin' Chicken is a modified hot wing recipe that I like to do with a whole chicken and is great to take camping or for the backyard barbecue. The fresh herbs and the salt from the soy sauce make a great combo and change it up from your usual barbecued chicken.

1 Cut the chicken into 10 pieces. Set aside.

2 In a large bowl, combine the soy sauce, water, garlic, rosemary, thyme, cilantro, oregano, and jalapeño. Use a hand blender to pulse the mixture until smooth. Add the chicken and let marinate overnight. Drain.

3 Preheat the grill to medium heat and grill the chicken until golden brown and chicken is cooked all the way through (about an hour). Once browned, lay the chicken on tinfoil and let it rest for 10 minutes before serving.

Makes 8 servings

1 whole chicken

½ cup soy sauce

½ cup water

5 cloves garlic, minced

1 tablespoon fresh rosemary, chopped

1 tablespoon fresh thyme, chopped

1 tablespoon fresh cilantro, chopped

1 tablespoon fresh oregano, chopped

1 jalapeño, chopped

BRO' NOTE:

THIS IS ALSO A GOOD RECIPE FOR WINGS. AND FOR ADDED FUN, GLAZE THE CHICKEN WITH HONEY AT THE END, RIGHT BEFORE SERVING.

AT SEA SASHIMI

Well, after catching fish all day in the hot Hawaii sun, you are usually pretty hungry. Why not sample your catch by cutting into one of your small ahi and eating some At Sea Sashimi?

1 fresh-caught ahi

wasabi paste

soy sauce

1 Nothing tastes better at sea than fresh-caught, raw fish. Fillet the ahi at sea, and toss the guts overboard. Cut the fish into thin slices and dip in wasabi and soy sauce.

Makes 6 to 8 servings

BRO' NOTE:

YOU USUALLY WANT AN AHI TO SIT ON ICE FOR 24 HOURS BEFORE CUTTING AND EATING, BUT SOMETIMES—ESPECIALLY WHEN YOU'RE HUNGRY—YOU ARE ALLOWED TO BREAK THE RULES.

This omelet is huge. It really hits the spot after a long night of howling at the moon. I pulled this off after a camping trip to our favorite beach, where Travis and I ended up celebrating our birthdays (they're three days apart). This big ol' omelet fed the whole party. Good times.

1 Heat a large nonstick pan over a fire or camp stove to medium.

2 Crack the eggs into a large bowl and whip with a fork. Set aside.

3 Fry the bacon in the preheated pan until crisp. Add the onions and peppers, and cook until the onions are translucent.

4 Pour the whipped eggs into the pan with the bacon and veggies, and cook until the eggs are light and fluffy. Attempt to flip. (Remember: when you flip, you have to go all the way, or you're gonna end up with a scramble.) Once flipped, top with shredded cheese and fold in half. Cut into equal parts and serve.

Makes 15 to 20 servings

24 eggs

1 pound bacon, chopped

1 onion, small diced

1 green bell pepper, small diced

8 ounces shredded Cheddar cheese

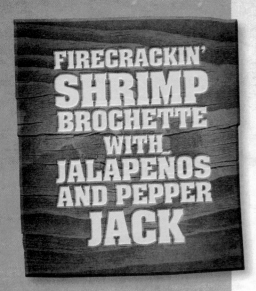

FIRECRACKIN' SHRIMP BROCHETTE WITH JALAPEÑOS AND PEPPER JACK

1 pound jumbo shrimp

4 ounces pepper jack cheese

2 jalapeños

1/2 pound bacon

It was love at first bite the first time I wrapped my lips around a bacon-wrapped shrimp, and when I decided to throw a little jalapeño along with some pepper jack in the mix, it was a hit.

1 Clean and devein the shrimp, and set aside.

2 Slice the cheese into 1 x 1/2-inch rectangles and set aside.

3 Slice the jalapeños into slivers. (The jalapeños will control how hot these shrimp turn out, so if you like it hot, give them a bigger slice of pepper.) Set aside.

4 If using wooden skewers, soak them in water 20 minutes before you're ready to skewer the kabobs.

5 Cut bacon slices in half and lay the slices on a cutting board, lengthwise. Place a shrimp, a pepper slice, and a cheese cube on each piece of bacon, making sure the bacon can completely cover the cheese and pepper on the big end of the shrimp. Wrap the bacon around the shrimp and place on a skewer. Repeat the process until there are no shrimp left.

6 Grill the skewers over medium heat until the bacon is crisp and cooked. Flip and cook for another 4 to 5 minutes or until the bacon is cooked and the cheese is starting to melt. Let rest and serve.

Makes 4 servings

BRO' NOTE:
YOU DON'T WANT TO OVERFLIP OR PLAY WITH THESE SHRIMP WHILE YOU'RE GRILLING BECAUSE IT WILL CAUSE THE BACON TO FALL OFF THE SKEWERS, AND THE SHRIMP WILL COME UNWRAPPED.

CAMPFIRE FISH STICKS

1 salmon, fresh
out of the river

1 (10-ounce) bag Louisiana
fish fry seasoning

1 squeeze bottle margarine

Who in their right mind would pack and carry a cast-iron skillet and a twelve-pack of beer three miles down a river to go camping? Our father, to answer that question. He had five of us little pack mules to carry all of the little extras those last couple of miles. We forgot all about having to slip and slide down the riverbank with that skillet once we started to catch and fillet fish. Those were the best meals ever, for some gratifying reason.

1 Fillet the salmon and then slice into thin pieces. Coat with fish fry seasoning. Fry in margarine over the fire. Serve and eat riverside. Salmon doesn't get much better than this.

Makes 6 to 8 servings

BRO' NOTE:

MAYBE IT WAS THE COLD, WET, AND HUNGRY FEELING THAT MADE IT TASTE SO GOOD.

Hiking camping trips are a little different from packing up your car and heading to your nearest campground. You have to learn how to pack light because everything you need, want, and desire is gonna be carried in on your back. I would suggest taking an herb butter or compound butter with you just in case you catch something to eat. Just so happens the river in Waimanu Valley was full of freshwater prawns, which were easily caught in the evening hours with a light and a spear. Shrimp scampi riverside in one of the most beautiful valleys in the world is very hard to beat.

WAIMANU VALLEY HERBED BUTTER SCAMPI

1 Before your trip, soften the butter. Add the chopped herbs, garlic, zest, and lemon juice. Mix well. Place in a zip-top bag and freeze until you're ready for your trip.

2 Spear or catch prawns in a prawn trap. Pull from the water and sauté them in the butter over a camp stove and serve. This tastes pretty good when you have been in the woods for a few days.

Makes 6 to 8 servings

½ cup (1 stick) butter

1 bunch parsley, chopped

½ bunch cilantro, chopped

3 cloves garlic, minced

juice and zest from 1 lemon

1 pound shrimp

BRO' NOTE:
I AM STILL SORRY I MISSED THIS TRIP. —TRAVIS

Quick and easy . . . meat in a can . . . What can I say? Think what you will, but I love the stuff.

1 Fry the Spam until golden brown and crispy. Remove from the pan and lay on a paper towel to absorb the grease.

2 In the same pan fry the eggs until over easy. Flip and add the cheese. Remove the pan from the heat and let it rest until the cheese melts.

3 Spread the mayo on the bread, top with the eggs and the Spam, and form your sandwich. Now it is time to grind!

Makes 1 serving

1 can Spam, sliced thin

2 eggs

1 slice Tillamook sharp Cheddar cheese

2 teaspoons mayonnaise

2 slices of your favorite bread

BRO' NOTE:

I'LL TAKE MINE EXTRA CRISPY . . .

POOR MAN'S LOBSTER

1 Boil the water with the sugar, vinegar, bay leaves, and onion for 5 minutes. Add the halibut and gently boil 10 minutes. Do not stir. Remove the onion and the halibut. Serve with melted garlic butter or cocktail sauce.

Makes 8 servings

8 cups water

1/2 cup sugar

1/2 cup vinegar

2 bay leaves

1 onion, sliced

2 pounds halibut

SOUPS AND MANWICHES

PRANKS ON THE BOAT: THE *SEABROOKE* EGGING

One thing about TV, no matter how hard you try, sometimes the epic proportions of a prank just can't be shown in a two-dimensional format.

One thing that comes to mind is our egging of Scott Campbell on the *Seabrooke*.

After finding the *Seabrooke* crest painted on the side of *Time Bandit*, we decided to retaliate with the biggest onslaught of eggs and make the biggest mess possible.

Mike Fourtner, Captain John, Captain Andy, and myself bought more than sixteen hundred eggs, enough to fill the bed of a full-sized truck to the bed rails . . . and set out recruiting additional people to help in what could be the biggest scramble in the history of the world.

We stopped by Original Productions' office to grab any possible help . . . then off to the *Northwestern* to grab Captain Sig and Nick Mavar. It was quite funny when the boat producer tried to tell Sig he had a meeting in thirty minutes and Sig was telling him to shut his mouth and stop thinking. He's the captain.

Upon arrival back at the boat, with an armada of people and sixteen hundred eggs, we throw the lines and make our way down the docks to where the *Seabrooke* is tied up, unaware of the egging just minutes away. We were lined up with people and eggs, and from where I was on the stern, it was ninety seconds before I was within firing range. And then the barrage didn't stop for about four minutes.

It was so ridiculously silly the amount of ammo we had that to get rid of all the eggs, we were throwing dozens at a time, covering the *Seabrooke* from bow to stern with at least half an inch of eggshells.

Because they didn't stand a chance, and we were going out to do helicopter shots for the episode intro, the *Seabrooke* crew didn't suspect anything, even with all the cameramen and the helicopter around. Go big or go home is what I always say, but that one was huge, and I'm not looking forward to paybacks on it.

Chicken Salad Pickle Sandwich

**Slap a Smile on Your Face
Ahi Salad Sandwich**

Crab Club with Vanilla Aioli

420 Philly

Garlic-Parsley Butter

4 Fathom Fish Stew

Crabby Chowder

**Rockin' Red Pepper Crab Bisque
with Cilantro Sour Cream**

For me, what really makes a sandwich is a crispy pickle, so for my chicken salad I like to use chopped pickles instead of dill weed.

1 Combine the chicken, celery, onions, and pickles in a large bowl. Add the mayonnaise, mustard, and salt and pepper. Mix well. Spread on one side of the bread. Top with lettuce and tomato slices and the other slice of bread.

Makes 4 servings

BRO' NOTE:

ON THE BOAT, FOR SAKE OF TIME, I USE CHICKEN OUT OF THE CAN, NOT TO BE CONFUSED WITH CHICKEN OF THE SEA . . .

CHICKEN SALAD PICKLE SANDWICH

Leftover chicken (white and dark meat), chopped fine

2 celery stalks, diced

1/2 onion, small diced

2 dill pickles, chopped

1/4 cup mayonnaise

1 tablespoon Dijon mustard

salt and pepper to taste

8 slices of your favorite bread or 4 croissants, split

lettuce and tomato slices

This is not an out-of-a-can tuna sandwich. Cooking in Hawaii, you get the opportunity to eat the freshest tuna, and when we have scraps or leftover cooked ahi, I like to turn it into tuna salad. And after the first bite, you will be slapped with that smile we are talking about.

SLAP A SMILE ON YOUR FACE AHI SALAD SANDWICH

1 Brush ahi steaks with olive oil and generously coat with kosher salt and coarse black pepper. Sear on a hot grill till medium. Cool.

2 Place the ahi steaks in a bowl with the celery, onions, peppers, capers, chili pepper, juice, and mayo, and mix.

3 Serve on toasted hoagie rolls with lettuce, tomato slices, and thinly sliced red onion.

Makes 4 servings

8 ounces ahi steaks, #2 grade

4 tablespoons olive oil

kosher salt, to taste

coarsely ground black pepper, to taste

2 stalks celery, finely diced

1/4 cup finely diced red onion

1/4 cup finely diced red bell peppers

2 tablespoons capers

1 Hawaiian chili pepper

juice of one lime

1/4 cup mayonnaise

hoagie rolls

lettuce

tomato slices

red onion slices

CRAB CLUB WITH VANILLA AIOLI

This sandwich is an old classic, but instead of cold cuts and bacon, we use crab, pancetta, and add a little vanilla aioli for an upscale version of the club.

1 To make the aioli: Combine the eggs, vanilla, and juice in a small bowl. Whisk in the oil and blend until smooth.

2 To make the sandwiches: Brush both sides of the hamburger buns with olive oil and toast under the broiler. Spread aioli on the bottom buns, place a slice of pancetta, a lettuce leaf, and a tomato on top. Add 2 ounces of crabmeat to each sandwich, drizzle with additional aioli, and add the top bun.

Makes 4 servings

Aioli:

2 eggs, room temperature

2 teaspoons vanilla

juice of 1 lemon

1 cup olive oil

Sandwiches:

8 slices soft white bread
or 4 hamburger buns

3 teaspoons olive oil

aioli, for spreading

4 ⅛-inch slices
pancetta, pan seared

4 leaves red leaf lettuce

4 slices tomato

8 ounces king crabmeat

BRO' NOTE:

SOUNDS AWESOME, BUT NO TIME FOR THIS ON THE BOAT.

420 PHILLY

This is a recipe that I made while attending chef school in Oregon. Me and a couple of friends opened a food booth at the annual hemp festival. We tie-dyed our chef jackets and sold 420 Phillys. Not a bad way to spend the weekend, and we made enough money to pay for all the beer we drank.

1 pound London broil

4 tablespoons olive oil

salt and pepper to taste

¼ cup butter

1 onion, julienned

1 bell pepper, julienned

6 cloves garlic, minced

2 ounces chopped fresh rosemary

½ cup Kahlúa

1 (14-ounce) can beef stock

1 baguette

garlic-parsley butter (from recipe below)

1 (9-ounce) package sliced Swiss cheese

½ cup shredded Parmesan cheese

1 Preheat the grill.

2 Baste the meat with olive oil. Sprinkle with salt and pepper. Set aside.

3 While the grill is heating, preheat a large saucepan over medium-high heat and melt the butter. Add the onions, peppers, and garlic and sauté. Toss in the rosemary and stir. Deglaze with Kahlúa and beef stock, and reduce the liquid over low heat.

4 Meanwhile, grill the beef to desired doneness, about 7 minutes per side for medium-rare. Let rest for 10 minutes before cutting.

5 Slice the beef thin and add to the onion mixture.

6 Preheat the broiler. Slice the baguette lengthwise, and cover with softened garlic-parsley butter. Place on a sheet tray and broil until golden brown.

7 Top the bottom side of the baguette with the beef and vegetable mix. Reserve the liquid for dipping. Top with cheese and broil till the cheese is melted. Serve immediately.

Makes 4 servings

1 In a small bowl combine the softened butter, garlic, and parsley. Refrigerate until ready to use.

BRO' NOTE:

TRAV: THIS IS ALSO ONE I PREPARE ON THE BOAT WITH LEFTOVER MEAT FROM TIME TO TIME. CROWD PLEASER.

1 stick butter, softened

2 cloves garlic, minced

1/4 cup chopped fresh parsley

4 FATHOM FISH STEW

This dish I learned working for my buddy Ron Gallaher at La Bourgogne, a cute little French restaurant that has lasted twenty-five years in Hawaii and is still going. This is a great dish that I would love to try with the fresh fish and shellfish of the Northwest instead of the farm-raised shellfish from Hawaii.

1 tablespoon olive oil

1 pound halibut, rockfish, or snapper

1/2 pound fresh mussels in shells

1/2 pound fresh clams in shells

1/2 cup (1 stick) butter

2 tablespoons diced shallots

1/2 pound shrimp, head on

1/2 cup small-dice zucchini

1/2 cup small-dice yellow squash

1/4 cup sweet corn

1/4 cup chopped red bell pepper

10 small pear tomatoes, halved

1 quart lobster stock

1 teaspoon saffron threads

1 tablespoon Herbs de Provence

juice of 1 lemon

salt and pepper to taste

tobiko (flying fish roe) and parsley sprigs, for garnish

1 Preheat the olive oil in a large saucepan over medium-high heat. Cut the fish into 4-ounce pieces and sauté. Set aside.

2 Rinse the mussels and clams, and debeard the mussels. Set aside.

3 In a stock pot, combine the butter, shallots, shrimp, mussels, and clams. Heat to medium; then add the zucchini, yellow squash, corn, peppers, and tomatoes. Stir to combine.

4 Add the lobster stock, saffron threads, Herbs de Provence, and lemon juice, and bring to a boil. Cook until the shellfish are open and cooked through. Add salt and pepper to taste.

5 Divide into four deep bowls. Top each with a sautéed 4-ounce piece of fish. Garnish with tobiko and parsley sprigs.

Makes 4 servings

BRO' NOTE:

TRAV: Okay, chef . . . sounds great, but for us non—culinary—trained folk, what are Herbs de Provence? Help a brother out here.

JASON: Herbs de Provence is a mixture of marjoram, thyme, oregano, rosemary, savory, and lavender.

CRABBY CHOWDER

Crabby Chowder is one of my favorite soups that the boys in the Bering Sea, I am sure, would enjoy after a long day of hauling gear. This is a little different from your traditional chowder because I add peppers and cilantro at the end, which gives it a unique flavor that everyone seems to enjoy.

1 Preheat the butter in a large saucepan over medium heat. Add the onions, celery, pepper, jalapeño, and garlic. Sauté until translucent. Add the flour and cook over medium heat for about 3 minutes, until the mixture has a nutty aroma. Add the clam juice, cream, and bay leaf. Bring to a boil and keep stirring until the soup thickens. Reduce the heat and let simmer for 45 minutes.

2 Turn off the heat and add the crabmeat and cilantro. Remove the bay leaf and serve with a nice baguette.

Makes 8 to 10 servings

3 tablespoons butter

1 onion, small diced

2 celery stalks, small diced

1 red bell pepper, small diced

1 jalapeño, seeded and small diced

2 cloves garlic, minced

1/4 cup flour

3 cups clam juice

1 pint heavy cream

1 bay leaf

2 pounds crabmeat

1/4 cup chopped cilantro

BRO' NOTE:

KNOCK YOURSELF OUT WITH THIS ONE. ONE THING MY BROTHER HAS REALLY HAD FUN WITH THE LAST SEVERAL YEARS IS GETTING CREATIVE WITH SOUPS . . . MUCH TO THE SATISFACTION OF MY BELLY.

ROCKIN' RED PEPPER CRAB BISQUE WITH CILANTRO SOUR CREAM

Cilantro cream:

1/2 cup sour cream

1/2 lime, juiced

2 tablespoons chopped cilantro

Bisque:

2 red bell peppers

2 yellow bell peppers

1 green bell pepper

1 onion

1 Anaheim pepper

1 jalapeño

7 tomatoes

3 tablespoons olive oil, divided

salt and pepper to taste

2 cloves garlic, minced

4 cups crab stock or water

1 cup heavy cream

1 pound crabmeat

Cilantro cream

Cilantro sprig, for garnish

Lime wedges, for garnish

It's kind of funny when you are blessed with some of the freshest seafood around and you get bored with ways to prepare your catch. Several years ago I was stumped on what to do with a bunch of fresh Dungeness crab. I'd been doing chowders, boiled crab, steamed crab, crab pastas, and all the other crab dishes you can think of, so I decided to let my fingers do some walking and look at recipes to get some ideas. The Rockin' Red Pepper Crab Bisque with Cilantro Sour Cream was a collaboration of several recipes, and it was a hit. When I told my brother Jason about it, he instantly made it as a special and sold out. Over the years we kept refining the recipe, ever improving the great flavors of the fresh vegetables with crab. I learned that having the right tools for the job cuts the time in half. Rule of thumb: don't use a blender, which is what I did the first several times making the bisque.

1 To make the cilantro cream: Combine the sour cream, lime juice, and chopped cilantro, and mix well. Refrigerate until ready to use.

2 To make the bisque: Cut the tops off of the red, yellow, and green peppers, clean out the seeds, and slice into 1-inch rings. Set aside.

3 Slice the onion into 1-inch rings and leave intact. Set aside.

4 Roast the Anaheim and jalapeño whole. Set aside.

5 Cut the tomatoes in 1-inch slices. Place in a large bowl and add the peppers, onions, and roasted hot peppers and toss with 2 tablespoons olive oil, salt, and pepper.

6 Grill until charred and slightly soft. Set aside.

7 Coat a large stockpot with 1 tablespoon olive oil. Over medium heat, roast the garlic till light brown. Add the roasted vegetables and the stock. Bring to a boil. Let simmer for 30 minutes.

8 Add the cream and mix with immersion blender or handheld blender. Garnish with crabmeat, cilantro cream, cilantro sprigs, and lime wedges.

Makes 8 to 10 servings

BRO' NOTE:

THE KEY TO THIS RECIPE IS GRILLING THE VEGGIES AND THEN PUREEING WITH A SOUP STICK (IMMERSION BLENDER). THE SMOKY FLAVOR FROM THE GRILLED VEGGIES PUT THIS BISQUE IN A LEAGUE OF ITS OWN.

LOSE-THE-BEER-BELLY SALADS

HEAD'S UP!

One night, after a forty-hour grind, the weather started coming up. I had Mongo pushing me to throw the hook on prospect pots, and pushing me to get to the table and sort crab. If I rested my hand on the table without a crab in the vicinity, it would get slapped. "Horn, you have two hands—use them."

All the while I'm reminded constantly how worthless and stupid I am from Blinddog. What always amazed me was how much these guys would watch me struggle for a while and then show me one little thing and my whole life would be easier.

I'll never for the life of me forget my first time walking out on deck in truly savage weather, walking down the companion way to the hatch to go outside. I'd look out the porthole and see a confused, whitewashed sea, then nothing but green water as a thirty-footer would roll by. Now, I don't know if any of you have ever stepped out into a total maelstrom or not, but you are so small compared to the raw power of Mother Ocean. It's quite humbling, actually. It's amazing how surreal everything is: the wind, the waves, the birds, the spray stinging your eyes, snow blowing sideways. There are a couple things I remember about that storm. I remember Mike looking at me and asking if I was scared, and if I wasn't, then I better get that way. Then opening the hatch, and Mongo, Dave, and Blinddog charging into the madness, screaming and hollering about anything in the book.

The other thing I remember very clearly hearing for the first time was "Heads up." I was cutting bait by the cod bin, glancing over my shoulder, 'cause a good rule is never turn your back on the water. There was one wave coming at us at a little different angle. It looked like it was going to hit the sea wall. I reach into the bin to grab a cod, and the next few events happen simultaneously: (1) Captain says, "Heads up!" (2) Boat makes a funny shudder. (3) I hear a great big smack.

I turned around to see nothing but a ten-foot wall of water headed my way like a freight train. Only three things came to mind: (1) *Drop the knife!* (2) *Get small.* (3) *Hold on, and hope for the best.*

Well, when the water cleared, Mongo was standing over me, moving a tote that decided to come to rest on me. As I hunkered down, Mongo said, "We're crabbing now, Horn." I was soaked from head to toe in thirty-four-degree water. The wind is blowing sixty miles per hour, and the outside temp is just below freezing. Wow. If that doesn't wake ya up, I don't know what will.

Now, that's happened several times since, some that have made TV shows, and in my opinion all of them are the same. Absolutely no fun at all, they can hurt, you're never dry, and most of the time the situation is "Pucker factor high." You know what I mean: when everything kind of gets real tight and puckers up. The moments when you say a prayer and see your life pass in front of your eyes. Nope, a pucker-factor-high moment is not fun at all.

The thing I remember the most from that night is it was the first time I'd ever been at sea and heard of a man overboard. Mongo comes into the gear room and tosses me a life jacket.

"What's this for?"

"Someone was lost off another boat about an hour ago. They haven't found him. Here. Put it on."

I can't even begin to tell you what went through my mind as I walked out on deck. That next string, the mood on deck was somber, to say the least. And it is definitely something that is in front of your mind. Thinking someone doing the same thing as you, seventy-five miles away, just lost his life. But what do you do? Just drive on! We continued working through the storm, and of course, in time the storm passed and it was business as normal. You know: scrambling, trying like heck to make everybody happy, which was a difficult job with the likes of one Blinddog.

But we'll talk more about him later . . .

Crab and Avocado Salad

**Blackened Halibut Caesar
with Lilikoi Butter**

**Fresh Greens with
Salmonberry Vinaigrette**

Making Miles Mac Salad

Cathy's Coleslaw and Dressing

This is another fusion-type dish, taking the crab that my brother (Travis) catches and using locally grown avocados to create a light but satisfying salad.

1 In a large bowl, combine the crab, aioli, chives, salt and pepper, parsley, avocados, tomatoes, curry, and lemon juice. Mix and mash until smooth but chunky.

2 Using a biscuit cutter, fill the inside of the ring with the avocado mixture to halfway. Lay a tomato slice on the avocado mixture, and then add another layer of avocado mixture (the biscuit cutter will help hold the ingredients in place and retain each serving's round form). Continue layering until the cylinder is full. Remove the cutter, and make the remaining salads the same way. Garnish with endives and chives.

Makes 4 servings

BRO' NOTE:

If you can pull off the presentation of this salad like my brother, you might as well call it the Seal-the-Deal Salad.

CRAB AND AVOCADO SALAD

1 pound king crab or snow crab, shucked out of the shell

1/4 cup lemon aioli (see recipe for vanilla aioli on page 64 and substitute vanilla with lemon)

1/4 cup chopped fresh chives

salt and pepper

2 tablespoons chopped parsley

2 ripe avocados, cut to medium dice

1 Roma tomato, diced

1 teaspoon curry powder

1 teaspoon lemon juice

fresh tomato slices

endive leaves, for garnish

chives, for garnish

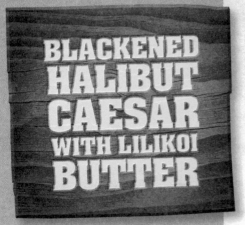

BLACKENED HALIBUT CAESAR WITH LILIKOI BUTTER

There is nothing better in my opinion than a nice piece of blackened fish on a crisp Caesar salad. I put my Hawaiian twist on it by adding a dollop of lilikoi butter to the fish, which cuts the heat of the blackened fish.

1 To make the Caesar dressing, place the eggs, anchovies, cheese, garlic, mustard, vinegar, lemon juice, and Worcestershire into the bowl of a food processor. Process slowly, adding the oil until you reach the desired consistency. Salt and pepper to taste. Refrigerate.

2 To make the lilikoi butter, place the juice, yolks, and sugar in a saucepan and simmer over low heat, continually stirring until the sugar dissolves. Add the butter and simmer, stirring occasionally, for two hours. Refrigerate.

3 To make the blackened fish, preheat a cast-iron skillet to very hot.

4 In a small bowl combine the paprika, cumin, garlic powder, onion powder, ground mustard, cayenne, black pepper, oregano, and salt together.

5 Coat the fish generously with the spice mixture. Add the vegetable oil to the skillet and cook the fish over high heat for about 3 to 4 minutes per side.

6 To make the salad, divide the lettuce among four plates or salad bowls. Garnish with the desired amount of croutons. Top with the fish, cheese, and lemon slices, if desired. Put a dollop of lilikoi butter on each slice of fish. Serve the salad with the Caesar dressing.

Makes 4 servings

Caesar dressing:

3 eggs, room temperature

1/2 (3-ounce) can anchovies

1/4 cup Parmesan cheese

5 cloves garlic

2 tablespoons Dijon mustard

1/4 cup white wine vinegar

1/4 cup lemon juice

1 dash Worcestershire sauce

2 1/2 cups vegetable oil

salt and pepper

Lilikoi butter:

3/4 cup lilikoi juice

4 egg yolks

4 cup sugar

2 cups (4 sticks) butter

Blackened fish:

1 pound fresh halibut, cut into 4-ounce steaks

1/4 cup paprika

2 tablespoons cumin

2 tablespoons garlic powder

2 tablespoons onion powder

1 tablespoon ground mustard

1 tablespoon cayenne pepper

1 tablespoon black pepper

2 tablespoons dried oregano or marjoram

3 tablespoons salt

1 tablespoon vegetable oil

Salad:

8 heads of baby romaine lettuce, chopped

croutons, for garnish

shredded cheese, for garnish, optional

lemon slices, for garnish, optional

When you are fishing on a thirty-five-foot halibut boat with no refrigerator out of Dutch Harbor, fresh vegetables are hard to keep fresh and looking good when you are moving your cold goods between iced fish holds and coolers.

It was a Sunday night, and we were gonna wait on a better forecast to avoid sitting on anchor, hunkered down and waiting out the oncoming storm. I had the great idea of having what I dubbed "Bartender Appreciation Night." Ya see, Sunday nights, the bar closes at 9:00 p.m., and believe it or not, you become great friends with the bartenders. This seemed like a great time to invite the girls over for dinner.

Just for fun, I did a couple of racks of ribs, twice-baked taters, and wanted to throw together a nice salad. To mix it up, I picked a gallon-size zip-top bag full of fresh salmonberries that I saw and mashed them up. Then I added garlic, basil, vinegar, olive oil, and Italian seasonings. Bam! A tasty dressing while tied to the dock.

1 To make the dressing, place the garlic, berries, vinegar, Italian seasoning, and salt and pepper in a food processor. Turn on and slowly add the oil until emulsified. Set aside.

2 To make the salad, in a large mixing bowl, combine the greens, cucumbers, tomatoes, onions, and peppers. Top with feta. Serve with the salmonberry vinaigrette. Serve with the Reckless Red Salmon and crusty bread for a great first course.

Makes 8 to 10 servings

FRESH GREENS WITH SALMONBERRY VINAIGRETTE

Dressing:

3 cloves garlic, minced

2 cups salmonberries or raspberries

1/4 cup balsamic vinegar

2 tablespoons Italian seasoning

salt and pepper to taste

1 cup olive oil

Salad:

2 large heads of romaine, cut into bite-size pieces

1 cucumber, sliced

1 pint cherry tomatoes, quartered

1 onion, thinly sliced

1 bell pepper, julienned

crumbled feta cheese

MAKING MILES MAC SALAD

1 In a large mixing bowl, combine the macaroni, celery, onion, bell pepper, olives, mayonnaise, and yellow mustard. Salt and pepper to taste. Stir well, chill, and serve.

Makes 15 to 20 servings

4 cups cooked macaroni

1 cup diced celery

1/2 onion, diced

1/2 cup diced green bell pepper

1 (16-ounce) can large black olives, sliced

5 cups mayonnaise

1/4 cup yellow mustard

salt and pepper to taste

CATHY'S COLESLAW AND DRESSING

1 In a large bowl, toss the cabbage, carrots, and onion. Set aside.

2 In a medium bowl, blend the sugar and the mayonnaise until the sugar dissolves. Add the Italian dressing and mix well. Stir into the cabbage mixture. Chill before serving.

Makes 15 to 20 servings

1 head green cabbage, shredded

1/4 head red cabbage, shredded

6 medium carrots, shredded

1/2 onion, diced

1/2 cup sugar

3 cups mayonnaise

1/2 cup bottled Italian salad dressing

SNAG-A-FIRST-DATE APPETIZERS

JUMPING SHIP

So one question everyone has is, "How did you get your job on the *Time Bandit*?" My normal response is, "Very carefully."

It all started when I began racing and the first sponsors I picked up were John and Andy, and then the *Time Bandit* race boat came about.

My intentions all along were to continue fishing on the *Wizard* and racing under the *Time Bandit* banner. But to do so I had to take the king crab season off, which I had seen happen several times with several other people.

One month prior to the season, I talked to Keith and I informed him I was going to take king crab season off. It was at that point he informed me he had just purchased two hundred new crab pots in Seattle and they had to be rigged before sailing across the North Pacific to Dutch Harbor, and to secure my job I had to fly out to Seattle and rig gear.

Well, it only took a couple of minutes to figure out that if I wanted to race in the World Championships in Key West, Florida, a trip to Seattle and a couple of weeks of time didn't fit into my plan.

So I called John Hillstrand, the captain of the *Time Bandit*, knowing they always needed an extra man for opilio crab season. After explaining the details of my plans and what was going on, I asked him if he still needed a guy for opilio season. He laughed and said they were making the call tomorrow but that if I needed a job, I was hired.

So that was that. I would lose my spot if I stuck to my schedule, but I was hired in just a matter of minutes on a boat I never dreamed of working on. Ya know, life is funny that way. You make a plan, stick to that plan, and the inevitable happens—that monkey wrench gets tossed in. But with a little adversity comes the opportunity to adapt and overcome any obstacle.

My decision to "jump ship" was a move made to chase my dreams and goals of the championships and a decision I'll never regret. Unless you count being first loser to the National Guard team. But there are no regrets, because the winning team destroyed their boat to beat us by five seconds. During the race we crashed at least six times without such a catastrophic ending . . . just sayin'.

And about that new job, I've walked the deck of many boats in my fishing career, but the fraternity of brothers on the *Time Bandit* is like no other—family to the core.

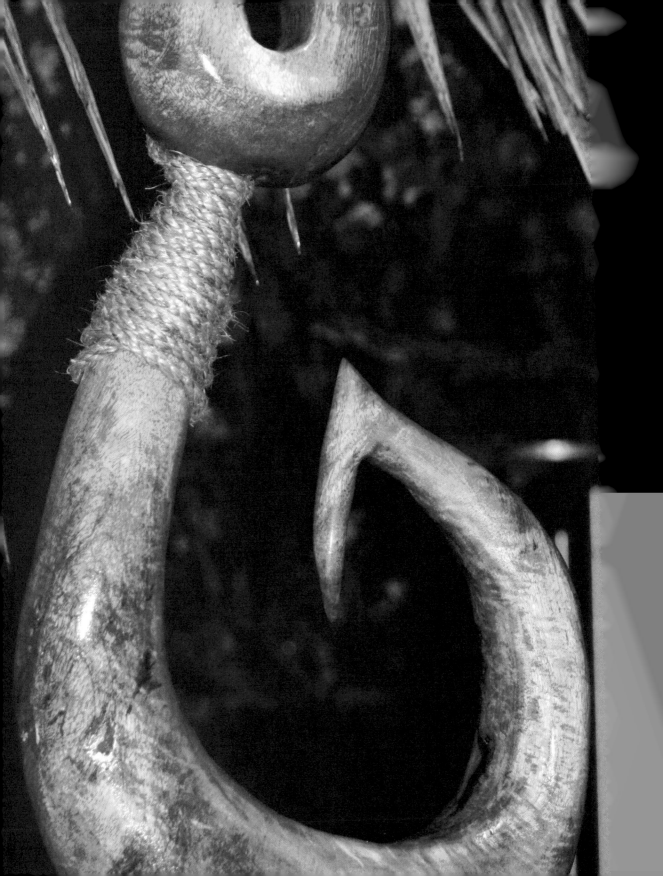

Salmon Log

Crab and Artichoke Dip

Crab-Stuffed Mushrooms

Sure-to-Impress Avocado Brie Melt

The King of King Crab Rolls

Crab Cakes

Crazy Crab Quesadilla

Mango, Papaya, and Brie Quesadilla

Honey Sesame Shrimp on the Barbie

Crab Poppers

Calamari

SALMON LOG

1 In a large bowl mix the salmon, cream cheese, lemon juice, onions, horseradish, salt, and liquid smoke. Roll into a log shape.

2 On a clean, dry surface, combine the pecans and parsley. Roll the salmon log in the pecans and parsley to coat. Chill and serve with crackers or as a sandwich filling.

Makes 10 to 12 servings

2 cups canned salmon

1 (8-ounce) package cream cheese, softened

1 tablespoon lemon juice

2 teaspoons grated onion

1 teaspoon horseradish sauce

1/4 teaspoon salt

1/4 teaspoon liquid smoke

1/4 cup chopped pecans

3 tablespoons snipped parsley

CRAB AND ARTICHOKE DIP

Crab and artichoke dip is a great first course or appetizer to take to a party. I created this after working a summer in Alaska at a lodge that my dad and I helped build before I headed to chef school. I then later worked in the kitchen, where we served a salmon artichoke dip that we sold constantly, which inspired me to try it with king crab instead. It worked.

1 teaspoon plus 2 tablespoons olive oil, divided

¼ cup chopped white onion

2 tablespoons minced garlic

¼ cup chopped red bell pepper

1 cup cream cheese

1 cup Parmesan cheese, divided

8 ounces king crabmeat, chopped

1 cup chopped artichoke hearts

¼ cup sherry

salt and pepper to taste

1 Preheat the oven to 450°F.

2 Preheat 1 teaspoon olive oil in a medium saucepan over medium heat. Add the onions, garlic, and bell pepper and sweat until the onions are translucent and some of the moisture is released. Cool.

3 Fold the cream cheese and ¼ cup of the Parmesan into the cooled vegetables. Add the crabmeat, 2 tablespoons olive oil, artichokes, and sherry. Salt and pepper to taste.

4 Place the mixture in a small casserole dish or soufflé cups. Top with the remaining Parmesan. Heat in the oven for 10 to 15 minutes until hot and bubbly. Serve with focaccia or crostini.

Makes 4 servings

BRO' NOTE:

TRAV: DUDE . . . COME ON. YOU REALLY WANT PEOPLE TO SWEAT AN ONION? WHAT'S THAT?

JASON: PUT IT IN THE SAUNA . . . GOOD THING YOU HAVE ONE ON THE *TIME BANDIT*. NO, SERIOUSLY, YOU COOK THE ONIONS OVER MEDIUM HEAT UNTIL THEY ARE TRANSLUCENT AND SOME OF THE MOISTURE IS RELEASED . . . DUDE.

CRAB-STUFFED MUSHROOMS

Well, have you ever heard the saying "Keep it simple, stupid"? With these fresh and quality ingredients, how can you go wrong?

15 button mushrooms

1 tablespoon olive oil

2 tablespoons butter

2 cloves garlic, minced

¼ cup sherry

1 pound crab, shucked

½ cup Boursin cheese

cayenne pepper, for garnish

1 Preheat the oven to 350°F.

2 Remove the stems from the mushrooms.

3 Heat the olive oil and butter in a large saucepan. Add the mushroom caps and sauté for 1 minute. Add the garlic, deglaze the pan with the sherry, and remove from the heat. Let cool.

4 In a large mixing bowl, combine the crabmeat and cheese. Mix thoroughly.

5 Generously stuff the 'shrooms with the crab mix. Bake for 10 to 15 minutes. Garnish with a sprinkle of cayenne.

Makes 6 to 8 servings

BRO' NOTE:

THE FIRST TIME I TRIED THESE, I WAS THINKING, *WOW! IS THERE FUNGUS AMONG US?*

My brother (Trav) is always calling me for recipe ideas, especially when he is trying to impress members of the opposite sex, or in other words, wine, dine, and have a good time. Here's a great one, bro.

SURE-TO-IMPRESS AVOCADO BRIE MELT

1 In a small bowl mix the sour cream, mayonnaise, and chipotle. Refrigerate until ready to serve.

2 Lightly brown the baguette slices under a broiler. Remove from the oven.

3 Top each baguette slice with avocado slices, 1 tablespoon of the sour cream mixture, and a slice of Brie and melt under the broiler.

4 Great as a first course for Reckless Red Salmon.

Makes 8 servings

½ cup sour cream

½ cup mayonnaise

1 chipotle pepper in adobo sauce, chopped

1 baguette, sliced ½-inch thick at a bias

2 avocados, sliced

1 Brie wheel, sliced into 8 slices

BRO' NOTE:

HA-HA. HE'S GIVING AWAY ALL MY SECRETS. ALWAYS QUICK TO THROW ME UNDER THE BUS . . .

THE KING OF KING CRAB ROLLS

Rice:

6 cups calrose or sushi rice

6 cups water

Vinegar:

2/3 cup rice vinegar

1 cup sugar

2 tablespoons salt

Sushi:

1 package nori sheets

1 pound king crabmeat

1 cup cream cheese

1 cucumber, julienned or shredded

1 bunch scallions

cayenne pepper or Hawaii chili pepper

I (Jason) have been lucky enough to have a brother who shows up with a box of fresh Alaskan king crab now and again. He is fortunate enough to have a brother who can roll sushi.

1 To prepare the rice, rinse the rice and drain well. Place in a large saucepan, add the water, and let it rest for 30 minutes. Then cook the rice for 20 to 30 minutes. Drain and pour into a nonmetal container. Refrigerate.

2 To make the vinegar, pour the vinegar into a small saucepan. Add the sugar and salt, and heat until both are dissolved. Cool.

3 Pour the sushi vinegar over the rice and stir gently to mix in. Don't smash the rice.

4 Fill a small bowl with warm water and set aside.

5 To roll the sushi, lay the nori sheets on a bamboo mat and spoon a thin layer of rice on top. Dip your fingers in the water and press gently on the rice to get a nice, even layer. Add the crab, cream cheese, cucumbers, and scallions in a single layer in the middle of the rice. Sprinkle with cayenne. Use the bamboo mat to help you roll the sushi. Seal and slice into eight pieces. It's a good idea to dip your knife in the warm water between slices to keep the rice from sticking and falling apart. Keep going until you run out of ingredients. Serve with wasabi and soy sauce.

Makes 10 servings

Well, everyone loves crab cakes, and they are usually done with crab out of a can. In my opinion the best food is fresh food, and making crab cakes with fresh opilio (snow crab) is the only way to go.

CRAB CAKES

1 Preheat the butter in a medium saucepan over medium-high heat. Add the garlic, onions, bell and jalapeño peppers, and parsley. Sauté until the onion and peppers soften. Add the white wine and deglaze the pan, scraping any bits of vegetables off the bottom of the pan. Remove the pan from the heat and cool. Pour into a large bowl. Add the crabmeat, oil, eggs, cheese, Old Bay seasoning, 3/4 cup of the breadcrumbs, and salt and pepper. Mix well.

2 Cover your working surface with the remaining breadcrumbs.

3 On the dusted surface, form the crab mixture into 4-ounce balls. Flatten into patties.

4 Preheat about a 1/4-inch of oil in a cast iron skillet over medium heat. Add the crab cakes, being careful not to crowd the pan, and cook until golden brown on both sides. Serve with cocktail (recipe on page 199) or tartar sauce (recipe on page 198), your preference.

Makes 8 servings

2 tablespoons butter

2 cloves garlic, minced

1/2 onion, diced

1 red bell pepper, small dice

1/2 jalapeño, finely chopped

2 tablespoons chopped parsley

white wine (for deglazing the pan)

1 pound snow crabmeat

1/4 cup vegetable oil, plus more for frying

2 eggs, room temperature

1/2 cup Parmigiano-Reggiano cheese

1 tablespoon Old Bay seasoning

1 cup breadcrumbs, or your favorite cracker crumbs, divided

salt and pepper to taste

BRO' NOTE:

THIS IS A GREAT FIRST COURSE, OR YOU CAN FORM BIGGER PATTIES AND PUT ON A SANDWICH.

CRAZY CRAB QUESADILLA

When in doubt and out of time or ideas, I always throw together a quesadilla. You can't go wrong with crab and cream cheese.

6 ounces cream cheese

1 chipotle pepper in adobo sauce, chopped

1 bunch cilantro, chopped

juice from 1 lime

8 flour tortillas

8 ounces shredded sharp Cheddar cheese

1 pound crabmeat

3 tablespoons vegetable oil

1 In a large bowl mix the cream cheese, chipotle, cilantro, and lime juice. Spread ⅛ of the mixture generously on a tortilla. Top with Cheddar cheese and crabmeat. Fold and cook over medium heat on a well-oiled cast iron skillet. Cook till golden brown, and then flip. Repeat with the remaining tortillas. Serve with sour cream and your favorite salsa or pico de gallo.

Makes 8 servings

BRO' NOTE:

THIS IS PERFECT FOR FOOTBALL PUPUS.

MANGO, PAPAYA, AND BRIE QUESADILLA

This recipe came from a friend and coworker who rattled this off in the kitchen one day when we were in a crazy quesadilla conversation. I ended up making it at my current job for a special during mango season. If this is on the special board, I don't have to worry about selling anything else, 'cause this is a winner.

½ wheel Brie cheese, sliced thin

8 flour tortillas

1 cup shredded Cheddar cheese

½ papaya, sliced

½ mango, sliced

½ bunch cilantro, chopped

3 tablespoons vegetable oil, divided

1 Lay three slices of Brie on a tortilla; then layer with a spoonful of Cheddar cheese, papayas, mangoes, and cilantro. Fold in half. Add 1 tablespoon vegetable oil to a cast-iron skillet over medium heat. Place the folded tortilla in the pan and cook until golden brown. Flip and cook until the cheese is melted. Repeat with the remaining tortillas. Cut each quesadilla into four pieces and serve with your favorite salsa and sour cream or guacamole.

Makes 8 servings

BRO' NOTE:

THIS IS AN UPSCALE QUESADILLA. THE BRIE CHEESE GOES TOGETHER PERFECTLY WITH MANGOES AND PAPAYAS, WHICH GROW IN THE BACKYARD HERE IN HAWAII.

1 In a small bowl whisk together 4 tablespoons sesame oil, sherry, soy sauce, honey, Sriracha, Chinese Five Spice, garlic, ginger, scallions, and sesame seeds, and pour over the shrimp. Marinate for 30 minutes.

2 Remove the shrimp to a bowl and toss it in the remaining sesame oil.

3 Pour the marinade in a saucepot and reduce until syrupy. Use as a glaze to baste the shrimp as you barbecue them.

4 Preheat the grill. Set a grill pan over medium-high heat.

5 Add the shrimp to the grill and cook 2 to 3 minutes. Flip and cook another minute on the other side. Baste the shrimp with the hot marinade and grill for 1 minute more. Remove from the grill and serve.

Makes 8 appetizers

HONEY SESAME SHRIMP ON THE BARBIE

5 tablespoons dark sesame oil, divided

3 tablespoons sherry

3 tablespoons soy sauce

1½ tablespoons honey

1 tablespoon Sriracha (Asian hot sauce)

½ teaspoon Chinese Five Spice powder

2 cloves garlic, crushed

2 ¼-inch slices ginger

2 scallions, chopped

1½ tablespoons sesame seeds

1 pound shrimp

1 Preheat the oven to 400°F.

2 Slice the jalapeños in half, lengthwise. Remove the pith and the seeds. Set aside.

3 In a small bowl mix the crabmeat, cheeses, and paprika. Stuff the mixture into the jalapeno halves, and then wrap each pepper half with bacon. Place on a sheet pan and bake for 10 minutes or until the bacon is crispy and the cheese is melted.

Makes 8 appetizers

CRAB POPPERS

4 jalapeños

4 ounces shucked crabmeat

4 ounces cream cheese

4 ounces shredded sharp Cheddar cheese

1 teaspoon smoked paprika

4 slices bacon, cut in half

BRO' NOTE:

IF YOU'RE BRAVE, YOU CAN COOK THESE ON THE GRILL OR SMOKER OVER LOW HEAT, BUT IT IS A BIT TRICKY.

1 Cut calamari into 1/4-inch-wide strips. Set aside.

2 In a large bowl mix the egg, milk, and salt and pepper. Add the calamari and soak for 3 minutes.

3 Remove the calamari from the egg mixture and dip the strips in the cornflake crumbs to coat. Set aside.

4 Heat the oil in a wok to frying temperature. Fry the calamari strips just until golden brown. (If overcooked, calamari will get tough.)

Makes 4 servings

CALAMARI

1 pound calamari, cleaned

1 egg

1 cup milk

salt and pepper to taste

1 1/2 cups cornflake crumbs

3 cups vegetable oil

"TUCK IN YOUR SHIRT, BUT DON'T BOTHER WITH THE TIE" ENTREES

BLINDDOG

Blinddog. Now, there's a story within itself. He, to me, to this day, is the epitome of a grumpy, ornery crabber. His thought process on training a greenhorn was to belittle, taunt, and humiliate you into quitting so he could make more money. He truly enjoyed making your life miserable and took some sort of sick pride in it.

The reason for the nickname was his Coke-bottle-thick glasses, and without them he was truly blind. Well, coming from a military background, I had a full understanding of the break-you-down-and-build-you-up concept of training. I just let his remarks roll off, until one particular night his comments struck a chord. And there comes a point in a young man's life where calling someone out is in order.

We had been grinding for close to forty hours. The weather was average for the Bering Sea. Twenty-mile-per-hour winds, twelve- to fifteen-foot seas. Just another day at the office, right?

Well, it was up to the point of a wave grabbing the pot and hurling Blinddog and me off toward another little sea wall. I let go to fight another day. Blinddog didn't let go.

I don't know. Maybe life and limb are worth the bodily harm one can inflict upon himself to make his $5\frac{1}{2}$ percent of the 350 crabs in the pot, but I know my 2 percent of that pot could have waited forty-five seconds to put the pot back in the water, let it settle, and continue on. Just saying, I love my free-working parts. As I've already been beat down, it just makes more sense not to kick my own butt.

Well, Blinddog jumps up and graciously reminds me that I don't know anything. I'm stupid and pretty much worthless. And *then* the comment that, quite honestly, put me over the edge: "I hope you die."

Well, that's all it took.

Sometimes in life it's better to let people kick their own rears. Here he comes, tossing clubs in the air, missing wildly. So I grab him by his rain gear as he's charging me. Bend at the knees, take his energy, put my knees to his torso, and toss him halfway across the deck.

Now, I don't want to lose my job, so I'm not going to throw any punches. But he comes again. And this time I let him kick his own rear on the sorting table with a little toss.

By this time the captain is shouting, "Break it up!" and Mongo the deck boss is telling everyone to let it go, because this butt-whupping has been a long time coming. It was more like a wrestling match, because I wasn't throwing any punches, and he wasn't landing any—probably because he broke his glasses at some point in trying to kick my rear and couldn't see anything.

It was about the time the captain got between us that Blinddog actually landed a punch. Nice shot. As Captain Monte separated us, he sent Blinddog in to make a meal.

"That's it. We're shutting down for a couple of hours. Horn, you stay out here and clean up the deck."

So the deck clears, and I spend the next forty-five minutes cleaning the deck and cooling off.

All I could imagine was walking into a hamburger or sandwich or something

Blinddog had put a little present in. Instead I walk into Blinddog, and he's got taped-together glasses, a swollen elbow, spaghetti on the stove, and a handshake for me.

"Horn, you got some fire in ya; I like that."

From that point on I was *still* Horn, but the BS stopped.

My initiation into the Bering Sea brotherhood was coming along nicely. I stunk like bait. I couldn't sleep the four hours allocated nightly due to my hands falling asleep and cramping and not cooperating for the first two hours of my twenty-four-hour day. I'd been pummeled by waves, ridiculed by the full-share guys, and now my archnemesis had befriended me because I helped him kick his own rear. Just used his energy to do it. Cool. This is exactly what I expected, right? I left my job bartending in Austin, college courses, and chasing cuties . . . for *this*?

Yeah. I was livin' now.

Hot Hawaiian Nights Pizza

Grilled King Crab Pizza

Pale Ale Pizza Dough

Rosemary-Pressed Ribeye

Grilled Filet with Lemon Tamari Butter

New York Steak with Ponzu Sauce

Grilled Tri-Tip with Gorgonzola
Pepper Cream Sauce

Grilled Salmon with Herb Butter

Reckless Red Salmon

Four-Cheese Halibut

Clam Linguine

Blackened Fish Tacos

Sweet Onion Battered Halibut

Coffee-Rubbed Beef Brisket

Wonton-Crusted Ahi with Ponzu Sauce

Grilled Salmon with Wax
On, Wax Off BBQ Sauce

Leftover BBQ Chicken Pizza

Our father has built a stone pizza oven in his yard, giving us the chance to experiment and make pizza and bread the way it is supposed to be. This is my version of my favorite Hawaiian pizza, with Canadian bacon and pineapple, and for fun we add fresh, sliced jalapeños, which balances well with the sweet from the pineapple.

1 Prepare the pizza dough and refrigerate until ready to use (your dough can be made up to a day ahead).

2 In a small bowl mix the tomato paste, garlic powder, Italian seasoning, salt, and pepper. Refrigerate for 1 hour while you prep your toppings.

3 Remove the dough from the fridge and let it sit for a half hour.

4 Preheat the oven to 450°F.

5 Roll out the dough on a well-floured surface and shape it to match your pizza pan. (If you don't have a pizza pan, a cookie sheet will work.)

6 Grease the pizza pan, and place the dough in the pan. Cover with the tomato paste mixture. Add the cheeses, bacon, pepper, and pineapple chunks. Bake on the middle rack of the oven for 10 to 15 minutes.

7 Remove the pizza from the oven and let it rest for at least 5 minutes before slicing. Enjoy!

Makes 8 servings

Pale Ale Pizza dough (page 120)

1 can tomato paste

1 tablespoon garlic powder

1 tablespoon Italian seasoning

1 teaspoon salt

pepper to taste

8 ounces grated mozzarella cheese

1/4 cup fresh grated Parmesan cheese

8 ounces Canadian bacon, sliced in strips

1 jalapeño, chopped

1 cup pineapple chunks

GRILLED KING CRAB PIZZA

It is one thing making pizza at home, but if you really want to impress your friends, try cooking it outside on your barbecue grill. Then throw some king crab on there. Our friends were skeptical at first when we told them we were gonna grill a pizza and weren't too sure about a pizza with crab on it. Once the first pizza came off the grill, I could not make them fast enough.

Pale Ale Pizza
Dough (page 120)

Pizza sauce:

1 cup cream cheese, softened

1/4 cup heavy cream

1 tablespoon olive oil

1/2 pound chopped spinach

5 cloves garlic, minced

Pizza toppings:

1 pound king crabmeat

1/2 pound chopped spinach

2 cups mozzarella cheese

1 cup Parmesan cheese

1 cup chopped green onion

1 Prepare the pizza dough, form the crust, and set aside.

2 To make the pizza sauce, combine the cream cheese and heavy cream in a medium mixing bowl and stir well. Refrigerate while you prepare the spinach and garlic.

3 Heat the olive oil in a medium saucepan over medium heat. Add the spinach and garlic and sauté until the spinach is wilted. Cool, and then squeeze out the moisture.

4 Fold the spinach and garlic into the cream cheese mixture. Refrigerate until ready to use.

5 Heat the grill to medium (make sure it is clean). Meanwhile, shuck the crab and get the toppings ready.

6 Spray the heated grill with nonstick cooking spray. Place the crust on the grill. Spread immediately with the sauce and top with the chopped spinach, mozzarella and Parmesan cheeses, green onions, and crabmeat. Quickly close the lid. Let the crust cook in the closed grill, checking occasionally to make sure it doesn't burn. If the crust is getting too done before the cheese has melted, remove from the grill and finish in a 350°F oven.

Makes 8 servings

BRO' NOTE:

THE FIRST TIME I ATTEMPTED THIS, I CONSTRUCTED THE PIZZA ON A PAN AND LOST HALF THE INGREDIENTS TRYING TO TRANSFER THE PIZZA TO THE GRILL. BE CAREFUL.

PALE ALE PIZZA DOUGH

2 packages active dry yeast

2 tablespoons sugar

1 cup cold beer

1 cup water

5 cups all-purpose flour, divided (plus additional flour for dusting)

2 teaspoons salt

2 tablespoons olive oil

1 In a large bowl whisk together the yeast, sugar, beer, and water. Let stand for 5 minutes.

2 Add 4½ cups of flour, salt, and olive oil, and stir to combine.

3 Dust the countertop or kneading surface with the remaining ½ cup of flour, and turn the dough out onto the floured surface. Knead until the dough is smooth and elastic (about 10 minutes). Roll into a ball and let the dough rise until it has doubled in size. Punch down and divide the dough in half. Form 2 balls. Dust with flour, and cover with plastic wrap.

Makes 2 (14-inch) pizza crusts

This is a trick I picked up while I was taking a summer off of fishing and went back to work as a bartender at Troiani, a fine-dining Italian steakhouse in downtown Seattle. Chef Demo sat us down in a meat class during training and explained all the different cuts of beef we used and how they were prepared. The press sounded interesting, so I tried it out at the first opportunity to throw a steak on the barbecue, and in my opinion now, it's the only way to do a ribeye on the grill. All the marbling of the steak with the combination of smoke and rosemary make this a mouthwatering treat. By the way . . . don't do this steak the injustice of slathering it with steak sauce or cooking it to any point beyond medium-rare—leave it bloody as heck and it'll melt in your mouth.

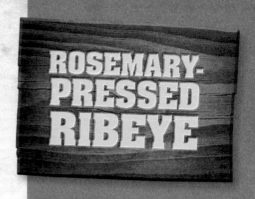

ROSEMARY-PRESSED RIBEYE

2 (1-inch-thick) bone-in ribeyes

¼ cup extra-virgin olive oil

cracked black pepper to taste

Kosher salt to taste

2 cloves garlic, minced

4 to 6 sprigs rosemary

1 Drizzle the steak with olive oil, and coat with the pepper, salt, and garlic. In a bowl, layer the rosemary, steak, rosemary, and the other steak. Refrigerate for 2 hours.

2 Preheat the grill.

3 Place the steaks on the grill at a 45-degree angle to ensure proper grill marks. Grill for 6 minutes per side for medium-rare. Serve with garlic mashed potatoes and steamed veggies.

Makes 4 servings

BRO' NOTE:

MY ONLY TIP ON THIS STEAK IS TO MAKE SURE YOU LET IT REST AFTER YOU TAKE IT OFF THE GRILL. LET IT SIT FOR AT LEAST TEN MINUTES SO WHEN YOU CUT INTO IT, YOU WON'T LOSE ALL THE JUICES. IT WILL MEAN THE DIFFERENCE BETWEEN A GOOD AND A GREAT STEAK.

GRILLED FILET WITH LEMON TAMARI BUTTER

The lemon tamari butter is my French Pacific Rim fusion that I created after seven years of cooking Pacific Rim cuisine in Hawaii hotels and then working in a fine-dining French restaurant. I took the favorite lemon and shoyu that the locals love on fish, steak, or just about anything and turned it into a compound butter that goes good on just about everything except ice cream.

4 (6-ounce) filet mignons

1 tablespoon olive oil

salt and pepper to taste

½ cup (1 stick) butter, softened

2 cloves garlic, minced

2 tablespoons tamari soy sauce

juice and zest of 1 lemon

3 tablespoons chopped cilantro

1 Brush the filets with olive oil and salt and pepper generously. Set aside.

2 In a medium bowl add the butter, garlic, soy sauce, lemon juice, zest, and cilantro. Whisk to combine. Wrap the butter in plastic wrap and refrigerate until you are ready to use.

3 Grill the steaks until they reach the desired temperature. Remove from the grill, top with the whipped butter, and let rest for 10 minutes. Serve with your favorite side.

Makes 4 servings

BRO' NOTE:

INSTEAD OF CALLING MY CHEF BROTHER FOR ADVICE FROM THE MAINLAND ON IDEAS TO IMPRESS A LITTLE LADY—I MET THIS ONE WHILE SHE WAS ON VACATION, AND I WAS ACTUALLY HOME ON THE ISLAND—I MADE RESERVATIONS AND HAD MY BROTHER JUST FEED US WHILE WE SHARED A BOTTLE OF WINE, AND THIS IS WHAT HE FED US FOR OUR MAIN COURSE. CAUTION: THIS DISH WILL MAKE YOU FALL IN LOVE ON A FIRST DATE! PROCEED WITH CAUTION.

NEW YORK STEAK WITH PONZU SAUCE

I learned this steak marinade from an eighty-year-old Japanese woman who prepared dinner for us while we were putting a roof on her house. It was the best steak I had ever had, and I have used it ever since. This was way before chef school, and since then I have added the ponzu sauce, which makes it a top seller in Hawaii.

4 (2-inch-thick) New York strip steaks

1/2 cup Kikkoman tempura dipping sauce

salt and pepper to taste

1 Coat the steak with the sauce. Let marinate for 2 or more hours. Salt and pepper to taste.

2 Preheat the grill.

3 Place the steaks on a piping hot grill and cook to the desired temperature. Top with Ponzu Sauce (recipe below) and serve with lemongrass wild rice pilaf and grilled tomato and scallions.

PONZU SAUCE

1/4 cup tamari or dark soy sauce

juices of 1 lemon and 1 lime

1/2 teaspoon garlic chile sauce

1 teaspoon mirin

1 teaspoon water

1 teaspoon cornstarch

1 In a small saucepan over low heat, combine the tamari, lemon and lime juice, chile sauce, mirin, water, and cornstarch, and bring to a boil. Cook until thickened.

Makes 4 servings

BRO' NOTE:

YOU CAN'T FIND TEMPURA SAUCE IN ALL STATES—BELIEVE ME, I'VE TRIED. THIS IS ONE OF MY FAVORITES TOO. YOU CAN IMPROVISE WITH A LITTLE SOY SAUCE, FISH SAUCE, BROWN SUGAR, AND A SMALL DASH OF BALSAMIC VINEGAR FOR YOUR MARINADE.

There is always more flavor in the tougher cuts of meat. This is pretty much a pepper steak kicked up with a little rich Gorgonzola cheese. One of the first times I made this congac cream sauce, I was working in a French restaurant in Hawaii. I would use a bottle with a speed top on it and the bottle was just about empty. When I poured the brandy into the pan and it began to run out, the fumes caught on fire, turning the bottle into a mini jet engine shooting the remainder of sauce and brandy onto the wall in a fiery inferno that scared the crap out of me and everyone in the kitchen. The fire was out as fast as it was lit but was a definite learning experience. When you're down to the end of the bottle, beware of the flameup, and take the speed pour off.

GRILLED TRI-TIP WITH GORGONZOLA PEPPER CREAM SAUCE

salt and pepper to taste

1 pound tri-tip

2 tablespoons vegetable oil

1 tablespoon butter

2 cloves garlic, minced

1 tablespoon freshly ground black pepper

1/4 cup brandy or your favorite whiskey

1/4 cup veal or beef stock

3/4 cup heavy cream

1/2 cup crumbled Gorgonzola cheese

1 Heat a skillet over medium-high heat.

2 Salt and pepper the meat generously. Add the oil and tri-tip to the preheated pan and cook for about 5 minutes per side, depending on thickness. (This cut is best served rare.) Leaving the burner on, remove the meat to a plate and let it rest for 10 minutes.

3 In the same pan add the butter, garlic, and pepper. Remove the pan from the heat, add the brandy, and place back on the heat. Deglaze with brandy and let the alcohol cook off. (Be careful, 'cause it will flame up.)

4 Add the stock and cream and let it reduce by half. Your sauce should become somewhat thick at this point.

5 Remove from the heat and stir in the cheese. Serve over the tri-tip. (Remember, this is a very rich sauce, and a little goes a long way.)

Makes 4 servings

BRO' NOTE:
THE FLAME IS IMPRESSIVE FOR GUESTS, BUT TRY NOT TO BURN THE HOUSE DOWN.

GRILLED SALMON WITH HERB BUTTER

This recipe is very simple, and if you have the opportunity to fillet a salmon you just pulled out of the water and cook it river- or oceanside, this is a simple way to make it great and impress any guest. You can have this herb butter prepared ahead of time so there is more time for fishing.

1 cup (2 sticks) butter, softened

salt and pepper to taste

4 cloves garlic, minced

1 tablespoon chopped fresh rosemary

1 tablespoon chopped fresh marjoram

1 tablespoon chopped fresh thyme

1 fresh Alaskan salmon, cut into four fillets

¼ cup olive oil

1 tablespoon chopped fresh flat-leaf parsley

1 In a small bowl blend the butter with the salt and coarsely ground black pepper. Fold in the garlic, rosemary, marjoram, and thyme. Refrigerate until ready to serve.

2 Preheat the grill till nice and hot.

3 Brush the salmon with olive oil, coating generously, and place the salmon at a 45-degree angle, skin side up. Establish grill marks and flip. Reduce the heat to low or medium heat. Cover and cook for 7 to 10 minutes depending on the thickness of the fish.

4 To serve, top with the softened herb butter and sprinkle with parsley. Serve with roasted red potatoes and grilled veggies.

Makes 4 servings

BRO' NOTE:

THE DIFFERENCES IN FLAVOR BETWEEN WILD-CAUGHT ALASKAN SALMON AND FARM-RAISED FISH . . . NO COMPARISON. PEOPLE OFTEN DON'T REALIZE THAT FISH FARMS ADD FOOD COLORING TO THE FISH MEAL TO MAKE THE FLESH A SALMON COLOR-OR THE NEGATIVE EFFECTS THE FARMED FISH BRING TO THE PACIFIC WITH HIGHER PARASITE LEVELS DUE TO THE AMOUNT OF FRY IN NET PENS-OR THE EFFECTS OF ESCAPED FISH THAT OVERRUN STREAMS, KILLING OFF THE NATIVE PACIFIC SALMON. IF YOU THINK FARM-RAISED ATLANTIC SALMON ARE SAVING THE WORLD, THINK AGAIN. SUPPORT SUSTAINABLE FISHERIES.

RECKLESS RED SALMON

1 cup grated coconut
¼ cup chopped cilantro
1 jalapeño, chopped
juice of 1 lime
salt and pepper to taste
1 sockeye salmon
fillet (skin on)

Serving suggestions: a BBQ, great friends, a full cooler, and Reckless Kelly on the radio.

On a trip to Austin after my first salmon season, I ran into some old friends: Kody, Willie, Naz, and Shifty, a.k.a. the band Reckless Kelly. They had just finished up a gig on Sixth Street and told me to stop by for a barbecue the next day. Given my past experience, this would be a South Park party (a type of party that the boys hold when they are not on the road and we fire up the barbecue and watch *South Park*), so I knew the food would be great. My contribution would be fresh wild Alaskan salmon.

Having grown up in northwest Washington and in Alaska, I had many a recipe for salmon that rocked, but not as much as their Hick Rockers recipe. We cooked several fillets, and hands down, this was the #1 hit.

Just like any fish, salmon is best when cooked medium-rare to medium (the Japanese have been eating fish raw for centuries), and there's no need to kill it by overcooking it 'cause, as I've said before, it's *already dead*!

1 In a small bowl combine the coconut, cilantro, jalapeños, and lime juice. Mix well and season to taste with salt and pepper. Set aside.

2 Grill the fish to medium doneness. Cover with the coconut mix, and serve with spaghetti squash. Garnish with additional cilantro and grilled jalapeños.

Makes 4 servings

BRO' NOTE:

WHEN TRAVIS SHARED THIS RECIPE WITH ME I WAS A BROILER COOK IN TALKEETNA, ALASKA, AND RAN THIS FOR A SPECIAL. BEFORE EACH DINNER SERVICE WE WOULD GET THE WAITSTAFF TOGETHER TO TASTE AND LEARN THE SPECIALS. I RAN THE RECKLESS RED SALMON AND RECEIVED A KISS FROM EACH OF THE WAITRESSES—AND ONE WAITER. I THINK THEY LIKED IT!

This is a family favorite and is probably the most common way the Lofland family prepares halibut for cookouts or parties. It totally breaks all the rules of cooking because most chefs say you should never serve fish with cheese, but I beg to differ.

1 Preheat the oven to 350°F.

2 Grill the fish to give it markings, and place it in a baking pan. Set aside.

3 In a large bowl combine the cheeses with the mayonnaise and sour cream. Spoon on top of the salmon, and bake for 30 minutes until bubbly and golden brown. Serve with pasta or potatoes.

Makes 4 servings

BRO' NOTE:
SECONDS, PLEASE.

1½ pound halibut fillet

½ cup shredded Cheddar cheese

½ cup shredded Swiss cheese

½ cup shredded Parmesan cheese

½ cup shredded mozzarella cheese

1 cup mayonnaise

¼ cup sour cream

BRO' NOTE:

TRAVIS PROBABLY USES DRIED HERBS WITH THIS PASTA, BUT IF YOU HAVE ACCESS TO FRESH HERBS, IT WILL TAKE THIS PASTA TO A WHOLE OTHER LEVEL. ALWAYS REMEMBER THAT WHEN USING FRESH HERBS, USE TWICE AS MUCH AS YOU WOULD IF YOU WERE USING DRIED.

My mom and stepdad were caretakers of a small island in the San Juans, and I decided to go adventuring and get some steamer clams. Without a good steamer recipe, I called on my Italian friend Uncle Sal for this simple pasta recipe. On the boat I substitute the fresh ingredients with Italian seasonings and canned clams.

CLAM LINGUINE

1 Heat the oil in a large saucepan. Rinse the clams and add them to the saucepan. Let the clams cook for 1 minute; then add the garlic and shallots. Deglaze with sherry and cook off the alcohol. Add the clam juice, cook, and reduce till the clams open. Swirl in the butter. Add the parsley and marjoram, and toss with linguine. Top with the cheese (may substitute shredded Parmesan). Serve with garlic bread and a nice white wine.

Makes 4 servings

olive oil, for frying

1 pound fresh clams

2 tablespoons chopped garlic

1 tablespoon chopped shallots

3 ounces sherry

1/2 cup clam juice or broth

1/2 cup (1 stick) butter

2 tablespoons chopped fresh parsley

1 tablespoon chopped fresh marjoram

1 box linguine, cooked according to the package directions

4 ounces Parmigiano-Reggiano, shaved

BLACKENED FISH TACOS

Everyone loves blackened halibut, and I personally love tacos, or Mexican food in general. This recipe is a collaboration of something I (Travis) prepared on the boat and something we have made together several times, evolving into how we prepare it now.

1 pound rockfish or halibut

¼ cup Chef Paul Prudhomme's Blackened Redfish Magic seasoning blend

4 Roma tomatoes

¼ cup diced onion

1 jalapeño, diced (can add 1 tablespoon more if you like it hot)

¼ cup chopped cilantro, divided

3 limes

salt to taste

½ head cabbage

¼ cup sour cream

1 chipotle pepper

1 teaspoon sugar

8 corn or flour tortillas

1 Season the fish with the blackened redfish seasoning. Cover and refrigerate while you prepare the other components.

2 Dice the tomatoes and place in a large mixing bowl. Add the onions, jalapeños, and half of the cilantro. Add the juice of one lime. Season with salt to taste. Refrigerate while you make the slaw.

3 Slice the cabbage extremely thin and place in a large bowl. Add the sour cream, chipotle, sugar, the remaining cilantro, and the juice of the remaining limes. Mix, and let stand in the refrigerator for 1 hour.

4 Heat a cast-iron skillet or grill over medium-high heat. Cook the fish to medium doneness, and let rest for 5 to 10 minutes; then lightly chop. Serve in hot tortillas topped with the Mexican slaw and pico de gallo.

Makes 8 servings

BRO' NOTE:

WHEN I MAKE THIS ON THE BOAT, I USE TARTAR SAUCE AND SALSA FOR THE SAUCE FOR THE SLAW. A QUICK AND DIRTY FIX FOR ON-THE-FLY COOKING AT SEA.

SWEET ONION BATTERED HALIBUT

3/4 cup cold beer or lemon-lime soda

1 1/4 cup flour, divided

1 tablespoon salt

1 egg, beaten

1/4 cup cornstarch

1 pound halibut, cut in 1-inch strips

1 sweet onion, cut thinly on a mandolin or with a knife

4 cups vegetable oil

1 In a metal bowl mix the beer, 1 cup of flour, salt, egg, and cornstarch. Set aside.

2 Shake the fish and onions in the remaining flour to coat. Wrap the fish with the onion. Set aside.

3 Preheat the oil in a large stockpot to 350°F.

4 Dip the onion-wrapped fish in the beer batter; then fry in the hot oil for 5 to 7 minutes until the batter is golden brown. Remove from the oil and drain on paper towels. Serve with cocktail (recipe on page 199) or tartar sauce (recipe on page 198).

Surrounded by coffee farms where some of the best coffee in the world is grown, I have had the opportunity to use it a variety of ways. This is my favorite, mainly because I love grilling.

COFFEE-RUBBED BEEF BRISKET

1 Trim the brisket of excess fat.

2 To make the rub, in a small bowl combine the smoked paprika, coffee, brown sugar, cumin, coriander, salt, black, white, and cayenne peppers, and mustard. Rub the brisket generously with the mixture. Let sit overnight in the refrigerator.

3 To make the mop sauce, combine the vinegar, mustard, and salt in a small bowl. Refrigerate.

4 To cook the brisket, set up your barbecue for indirect grilling. Soak the smoke chips. Smoke the brisket for 2 hours, soaking with mop sauce when needed, reserving some sauce for topping. After 2 hours, wrap the brisket in foil and throw it back on the heat. Cook 3 to 4 hours, until the meat has shrunk in the foil. Remove from the heat and let it rest for 15 minutes in the foil. Then remove the foil, slice the beef thin, and top with remaining mop sauce.

Makes 10 servings

BRO' NOTE:

JUST FOR FUN, PUT WHOLE COFFEE BEANS IN WITH YOUR SMOKE CHIPS FOR ADDED FLAVOR AND COLOR.

1 (6–8 pound) brisket

Rub:

¼ cup smoked paprika

¼ cup kau coffee

¼ cup brown sugar

2 tablespoons cumin

2 tablespoons coriander

3 tablespoons salt

2 tablespoons black pepper

2 tablespoons white pepper

2 tablespoons cayenne pepper

2 tablespoons dry mustard

Mop sauce:

½ cup balsamic vinegar

¼ cup Dijon mustard

2 tablespoons salt

This is a special I created when I worked at the Sheraton. It is a definite crowd pleaser. The presentation is awesome, and it tastes good too.

WONTON-CRUSTED AHI WITH PONZU SAUCE

1 Preheat the oil in a fryer to 325° or 350°F.

2 Cut the fish into 2 x 2 x 4-inch rectangles. Set aside.

3 Slice the wontons as thin as you can and place in a metal bowl.

4 Place the flour in one bowl, the eggs in another bowl, and set up a breading station with the flour, eggs, and wontons.

5 Coat the fish with the flour, then the egg, and roll in the wontons. Place in the fryer and cook until the wontons are golden brown, 1 to 2 minutes. (Be careful not to overcook.) Remove from the oil and drain on paper towels.

6 Slice the ahi at a bias or a steep angle and serve with the ponzu sauce, sautéed spinach, and jasmine rice.

Makes 4 servings

4 cups vegetable oil

2 (3-ounce) blocks sashimi-grade ahi

1 package wonton wrappers

1/2 cup flour

2 eggs, beaten

ponzu sauce (see recipe on page 126)

GRILLED SALMON WITH WAX ON, WAX OFF BBQ SAUCE

1 salmon fillet

1/4 cup plus 2 tablespoons soy sauce, divided

2 tablespoons brown sugar

1 tablespoon minced ginger

1/2 cup ketchup

1/4 cup rice wine vinegar

1/2 cup oyster sauce

1 teaspoon Chinese Five Spice powder

1/4 cup honey

1 Thai or Hawaiian chile pepper

1 In a shallow dish or zip-top bag, marinate the salmon in 1/4 cup soy sauce, brown sugar, and ginger for 2 hours.

2 Meanwhile, combine the ketchup, vinegar, oyster sauce and the remaining 2 tablespoons of soy sauce, Five Spice, honey, and chile in a saucepan. Bring to a boil over high heat; then reduce the heat and let the sauce simmer for 30 minutes. Cool.

3 Preheat your grill to medium heat. Remove the fish from the marinade and place skin side down on the grill. Cook the fish with the lid on for 10 to 14 minutes depending on the thickness of the fillet and how you like your salmon cooked. When done, remove the fish from the grill, brush with the sauce, and let it rest for 5 minutes before serving.

Makes 4 servings

BRO' NOTE:

FISH CONTINUES COOKING AFTER YOU REMOVE IT FROM THE GRILL, SO IF YOU PULL THE FISH OFF WHEN IT IS MEDIUM AND LET IT SIT, IT WILL BE MEDIUM—WELL BY THE TIME YOU SERVE IT.

LEFTOVER BBQ CHICKEN PIZZA

1 Prepare the pizza dough and refrigerate until ready to use (your dough can be made up to a day ahead).

2 Place the tomato paste in a bowl and stir in the garlic, Italian seasoning, salt, and barbecue sauce. Let stand in the refrigerator while you prep your toppings.

3 Preheat the butter in a medium saucepan over low heat. Add the onions and cook until golden brown in color and caramelized. Set aside.

4 Roast the pepper over an open flame on the stovetop or on a grill until the skin turns black, rotating until all sides are blackened. Place in a gallon-size zip-top bag, seal, and set aside to cool. Remove from the bag and remove the skin. Slice into strips.

5 Preheat the oven to 450°F and grease your pizza pan.

6 Roll out the dough on a well-floured surface. Spread a generous layer of sauce; then add the cheeses, peppers, and chicken. Sprinkle with the rib rub. Throw in the oven and bake for 10 to 15 minutes. Remove from the oven when the cheese is brown and bubbly.

Makes 8 servings

Pale Ale Pizza Dough (recipe on page 120)

1 can tomato paste

1 tablespoon granulated garlic

1 tablespoon Italian seasoning

1 teaspoon salt

1/4 cup of your favorite barbecue sauce

1 tablespoon butter

1 onion, julienned

1 red bell pepper

1/2 cup grated mozzarella cheese

1/2 cup grated sharp Cheddar cheese

Leftover Beer Can Chicken (page 10), pulled off the bone and torn into bite-size pieces

1 tablespoon Rub-a-Dub Rib Rub (page 193)

BRO' NOTE:

THIS IS PROBABLY THE BEST THING YOU CAN DO WITH LEFTOVER CHICKEN.

STARCHES AND SIDES

THE BIG WAVE ON THE *WIZARD*

You know that old saying "Everything happens for a reason"? Let's go with another old *Wizard* saying and that's "Hindsight is always 20/20." That's how I feel to this day.

It was opie season 2009. We had just had a thirty-plus-hour run to where we were going to set our gear. Being on a boat that ran twenty-four hours a day on a rotation, it came down to a cut of the cards between Art Peterson and myself on who was going to set the stack of gear and pull the first shift.

After a thirty-hour run, neither of us really wanted to go back to bed and would rather work the first shift, which meant guaranteed rack time in eighteen hours instead of tossing and turning the next six.

Art cut first and cut a 3 of hearts. It was looking good for me to work the first shift, when I cut a 2 of hearts. Art and I looked at each other and laughed and said, "Weird."

Back to the rack I went and tossed and turned, trying to crash out, then noticed the weather picking up. I'm not sure how long I slept, but I woke up being almost completely thrown from my bunk, the long way. I barely caught myself with my legs off of the foot of my bunk—the top bunk, no less. I pulled myself back up to my pillow and waited to spring into action if I heard the general alarm sound. Then I noticed there were no hydraulics running. Translation: the guys were not setting pots and were probably hunkered down, which, given the force of that last wave, would have been the place to be. Unfortunately, I've never been so wrong.

It may have been ten minutes and I hear voices in the hallway, which isn't uncommon. Usually it's *screaming*, so voices are no big deal. In walks Crosby, getting out of his wet gear, and asks, "Hey, bro, we just took a huge hit. We have some guys beat up."

I jumped out of the rack, asking what happened, and was it that huge

one, showing him how far I came out of my rack. He informed me that they were tarping the stack when that wave hit, and they were all lucky to still be on board.

What I didn't expect to see when I walked out of our stateroom was a triage-like situation. Lying at my feet is our second-year kid, Lynn Guitard, whose eyes said it all. You could see the dazed look of *How am I still alive?* Lynn had a cut above his eye and some bruises, but nothing compared to the shiner first mate and deck boss Soper had. He had a pack of frozen peas over his eye but seemed a little worse for wear.

Laid out on the galley floor, in obvious pain, was the Mouse, Monte Colburn, our producer. Doug Stanley was tending to him, and it looked as if he had broken ribs.

Back to town we went with the storm on our stern and the engine running, with no concern for fuel. We reached Dutch Harbor in nineteen hours to get our broken team to the clinic.

Once we got the guys to the emergency room, we took a look at the stack. The entire stack, three high, was shifted eighteen inches. Three sets of chains were supposed to hold the stack in place. It was evident that the tarp didn't allow the water to disperse, and the force caused the pots to shift drastically and blew the doors out of several pots. We're talking about twenty-plus tons of steel.

That whole hindsight thing, wow. We were lucky. Monte went home to mend his broken ribs. Soper flew to Anchorage to see if he had a fractured eye socket, and poor Lynn was stuck with us while we regrouped for our second attempt at our first trip.

There was definitely someone watching over us that day. We could have easily had six men in the water with only three of us aboard to rescue them, a situation that no one wants to be in. Broken bones heal.

Probably the best cut card in the stack that day.

Au Gratin Potatoes

Lemongrass Wild Rice Pilaf

Garlic Mashed Potatoes

Crazy Quinoa

Grilled Veggie Kabobs

Spaghetti Squash

Grilled Tomatoes and Scallions

Grilled Asparagus with Lime Vinaigrette

Grilled Corn on the Cob

Captain's Cornbread

Grilled Pineapple

Calico Bean Bake

AU GRATIN POTATOES

Who would have ever thought that I would have learned how to make scalloped potatoes from a Japanese guy? This is a simplified version of French potatoes au gratin that is a great addition to any meat dish.

1 Preheat the oven to 400°F.

2 Slice the shallots thinly.

3 Place the butter in a pan over medium heat. Add the shallots and sauté until slightly caramelized. Transfer to a mixing bowl.

4 Add the cream, thyme, salt, and pepper. Refrigerate until ready to use.

5 Peel the potatoes and slice thinly on a mandolin or with sharp knife. Place in a large bowl and toss with the cream mixture.

6 Spray an 8½ x 8½-inch square cake pan with nonstick cooking spray. Layer the potatoes in the pan, alternating with layers of cheese until all the potatoes are gone. Top with the cheese.

7 Cover with foil and bake for 45 minutes; then remove the foil and bake an additional 15 minutes or until the cheese is browned.

8 Remove from the oven and serve warm.

Makes 12 servings

2 shallots

1 tablespoon butter

1/4 cup heavy cream

1 tablespoon chopped fresh thyme

2 teaspoons salt

1/2 teaspoon white pepper

6 potatoes

nonstick cooking spray

8 ounces shredded Parmesan cheese

LEMONGRASS WILD RICE PILAF

1 Preheat the butter and olive oil in a small saucepan over medium heat. Add the rices and sauté until slightly browned. Add the onion and lemongrass and stir to combine. Add the broth and salt, and bring to a boil. Cover and reduce the heat. Simmer for 45 minutes or until all the liquid is absorbed. Let the rice rest, covered, for 5 minutes. Fluff with a fork before serving.

Makes 8 servings

2 tablespoons butter

1 tablespoon olive oil

3/4 cup brown basmati rice

1/4 wild rice mix

1/2 onion, chopped

1 (3-inch) piece lemongrass, crushed

2 cups vegetable or chicken broth

1 tablespoon salt

GARLIC MASHED POTATOES

I have had the opportunity to cook for and learn from chefs from around the world. While working the broiler station at a lodge in Alaska, I was in charge of preparing the starches for nightly dinner service. The one-eyed Swedish chef, Felix, tasted my garlic mash one evening and added a pinch of nutmeg that took my average garlic mash to a side dish that people will drive miles for, literally.

4 potatoes

2 tablespoons salt

½ cup milk

⅓ cup butter

2 teaspoons granulated garlic

1 pinch of nutmeg

salt and white pepper to taste

1 Peel the potatoes and place in a pot. Add enough water to cover the potatoes and stir in the salt. Bring to a boil and cook until tender. Drain.

2 Add the milk, butter, garlic, nutmeg, salt and pepper. Mash the potatoes with a hand masher until smooth. Keep warm until ready to serve.

Makes 4 servings

1 Melt the butter in a small saucepan over medium heat. Add the onions and quinoa, and sauté until the onions are translucent. Add the coriander and cook for 30 seconds, stirring to coat the quinoa. Add the chicken stock and bring to a boil. Reduce the heat, stir in the salt, cover, and simmer for 20 minutes until the liquid is absorbed.

Makes 4 servings

2 tablespoons butter

1/2 onion, chopped

1 cup quinoa

1 tablespoon coriander

2 cups chicken stock

1 teaspoon salt

GRILLED VEGGIE KABOBS

1 zucchini

1 yellow squash

½ onion

1 bell pepper

2 tablespoons olive oil

¼ cup rice wine vinegar

2 tablespoons chopped
fresh thyme

1 teaspoon kosher salt

1 teaspoon black pepper

1 Cut the zucchini and yellow squash in half lengthwise. Then cut each half into chunks. Cut the onion half in two. Cut the pepper into 1-inch pieces.

2 In a bowl, combine the oil, vinegar, thyme, salt, and pepper. Add the veggies and stir to coat. Marinate for 30 minutes.

3 If using wooden skewers, soak them in water 20 minutes before you're ready to skewer the kabobs.

4 To serve, place the vegetables on skewers, and grill until almost cooked through.

Makes 4 servings

SPAGHETTI SQUASH

1 spaghetti squash

½ cup water

¼ cup plus 2 tablespoons
butter, divided

1 tablespoon kosher salt

black pepper to taste

2 scallions, sliced

1 Cut the squash lengthwise into six pieces and remove the seeds and pulp.

2 Preheat the oven to 350°F. Place the squash skin side down on a cookie sheet. Pour the water around the squash. Slice ¼ cup of the butter thinly and cover the faces of the squash slices.

3 Bake for 20 minutes and remove from the oven. Turn the squash facedown and return to the oven. Steam for 45 minutes or until the squash is soft. Remove from the oven.

4 With an oven mitt or towel, grab the squash and use a fork to scrape out the flesh into a mixing bowl. Add the remaining 2 tablespoons of butter, salt, pepper, and scallions, and toss. Serve hot.

Makes 6 servings

GRILLED TOMATOES AND SCALLIONS

1 Cut the tomatoes in half. Cut off the ends off the scallions. Place the tomatoes and scallions in a bowl. Toss with olive oil.

2 Remove the vegetables and place facedown on a hot grill. Grill for 4 minutes and flip. Grill for 4 more minutes, season with salt and pepper, and remove from the grill.

3 Let the vegetables rest for 5 minutes before serving.

Makes 8 servings

2 tomatoes

8 scallions

2 tablespoons olive oil

2 teaspoons salt

1 teaspoon cracked black pepper

1 To prepare the asparagus, in a small bowl combine the olive oil, vinegar, thyme, salt, and pepper. Coat the asparagus with the mixture, and grill over medium heat for about 5 minutes on each side. Remove to a serving plate or bowl.

2 To make the vinaigrette, combine the lime juice, olive oil, salt, pepper, garlic, zest, and cilantro in a small bowl. Whisk until incorporated. Serve with the grilled asparagus.

Makes 4 servings

GRILLED ASPARAGUS WITH LIME VINAIGRETTE

Asparagus:

2 tablespoons olive oil

1/4 cup rice wine vinegar

1 tablespoon chopped fresh thyme

1 teaspoon salt

1 teaspoon pepper

1 bunch asparagus, root end cut off

Vinaigrette:

1/3 cup lime juice

1 cup olive oil

2 teaspoons salt

2 teaspoons black pepper

2 teaspoons garlic

zest of 2 limes

2 tablespoons chopped cilantro

GRILLED CORN ON THE COB

If you can get your hands on fresh sweet corn, this is definitely the best way to prepare it. You cook it with the husk on, which gives it the best flavor.

1 Soak the corn for 3 to 5 hours in salted water. Drain.

2 Preheat the grill to medium-high heat and grill the corn with the lid closed for 5 minutes. Flip and repeat until all sides are starting to turn black. Remove from the grill.

3 Remove the husks and smother the corn in melted butter.

Makes 4 servings

4 ears of corn

2 gallons water

1 teaspoon salt

½ cup (1 stick) butter, melted

BRO' NOTE:

SOAKING THE CORN IN THE WATER STEAMS THE CORN WHEN IT IS PLACED ON THE GRILL.

1 Preheat the oven to 400°F.

2 Grease a cast-iron skillet and place in the oven to preheat.

3 In a large bowl add the cornmeal, flour, sugar, baking powder, salt, milk, shortening, egg, corn, and pepper. Stir just until combined. Remove the skillet from the oven and pour the cornbread mixture into the preheated skillet. Bake 25 minutes until golden brown.

Makes 12 servings

CAPTAIN'S CORNBREAD

1 cup cornmeal

1 cup all-purpose flour

¼ cup sugar

3 teaspoons baking powder

½ teaspoon salt

1 cup milk

¼ cup shortening

1 egg

1 cup canned corn (optional)

1 jalapeño pepper, diced (optional)

GRILLED PINEAPPLE

1 large pineapple, peeled and sliced into ¼-inch rounds

¼ cup brown sugar

1 Preheat the grill to medium. Spray with nonstick cooking spray.

2 Grill the pineapple for about 3 minutes and then rotate 45 degrees and cook another 3 minutes to make grill marks. Flip and top with brown sugar. Let pineapple cook with the lid on for another 3 minutes. Remove from the grill and serve.

Makes 8 to 10 servings

1 Preheat the oven to 350°F.

2 Fry the bacon until crispy. Add the ground beef and onion, and cook until the onions are translucent. Add the ketchup, sugars, vinegar, mustard, and beans, and stir to combine.

3 Pour into a 13 x 9-inch pan and bake for 40 minutes.

CALICO BEAN BAKE

½ pound bacon, diced

½ pound ground beef

½ small onion, diced

½ cup ketchup

½ cup brown sugar

½ cup sugar

2 teaspoons vinegar

1 teaspoon mustard

1 large can pork and beans

1 (15- to 16-ounce) can kidney beans

1 (15- to 16-ounce) can butter beans

DESSERTS

MAN OVERBOARD

My second trip finished off like very few I've been on, with a disgruntled deckhand. Apparently he wasn't happy with the amount of crab we were catching. I picked up on this by watching his hand gestures and his not-so-quiet comments. I mean, if putting the gear on crab was as easy as parking the boat, then Dave would not be the guy to do that, given his performance tying up the boat prior to the season. Wow. Don't know how that one slipped my mind.

Captain Monte was in town on errands, and another boat was needing a little dock space to tie up. So Dave figured, no problem. Well, that fiasco I fondly look back on, and one song comes to mind. The circus song. Yep, a complete dog and pony show. Two greenhorns, a thousand hp, a million pounds of boat, sixty-mile-per-hour winds, and a dock guy whose English vocabulary was not sufficient for the task at hand.

We loosened the lines, Dave put her in forward, and away we went—although our dock guy didn't know he had to move the lines forward to the next cleats.

After thirty minutes of lots of screamin' by Dave, and several confused looks from a guy who's trying like mad to help us out but is handicapped by a language barrier, we get the boat secured to the dock, minutes before our captain arrives with a load of groceries and a confused look on his face, because the boat wasn't where it was when he left. Well, I guess Dave was lucky to not lose his job, but a captain is not going to stand for such blatant disrespect at sea. So yet another crew change. Doug, our one-and-a-half-armed chief, had the confidence in Mongo and Monte running the engine room, and stepped off, and here comes Mike Fitzgerald, great deckhand, my teacher, and the oldest guy on the boat, in his midfifties. Then the farmer—hair farmer, to be exact—a processor turned crabber, came aboard.

One thing that did happen that off-load was I got my first ever raise. I got called to the wheelhouse and Monte shook my hand and told me I was gonna get another one-half percent for a job well done and I deserved it. It's only happened twice in my career that I got a raise midway through a season, from Captain Monte and a few years later from his brother Keith, when I earned my full share on board the *Wizard*. I got called to the wheelhouse and got a bump in pay for a job well done.

I walked downstairs, trying to hide my excitement, after getting told I was not to mention it to the other guys. It was our business, and he cut into his pay to help me out.

Well, the first person I see is Mongo. He looks at me and says, "Why do you have that silly grin on your face, Horn?"

With a smirk, I replied, "No reason."

He asked me if I got a raise; I tried to lie, but to no avail. He then said the captain had pulled him aside and asked him how I was doing, in his opinion. He said he'd told him I was picking it up, and he felt I deserved a raise. Then he laughed and said, "I told ya to stick with me, kid."

So we set sail for the grounds and the start of our third trip. We hauled our first pot, chock-full of crab. Captain Monte's choice of fresh ground was paying off huge. I'm sure that, had Dave seen the full pots, he would have been eating his words. For the next week we worked our gear, hauling, moving, and hauling again, working the area until we got the call from Monte's brother Keith that he landed the gear on the mother lode, twelve hours away, and he was confident we had worked this area for all it had to offer.

We began stacking out and were gonna get our gear on the jackpot, unload, and come back out for another great pick to start off our fourth trip. It was business as usual, methodical putting of the gear on the boat. Spirits were high with the thoughts of full crab pots and a great finish to an already great trip, and then the thought of starting off our fourth trip with a bang.

We were getting close to finishing stacking our pot, with just three pots left, when the words "Man overboard!" rang out through the night. I looked up to see a pot swinging wildly on top of a stack and my mentor in the water.

The story of the next three and a half minutes will never be told, and the following eighteen hours looking for him after hypothermia took effect are a moot point. The outcome would have been the same: we had to return to port without one of our own and let down his family.

Upon reaching town I called my family in Alaska, since they were more than likely the ones to hear the bad news first. And I was right. My stepmother was watching the five o'clock Anchorage news when the story was aired. The story was just "A Seattle man was lost today off the *Seafisher*. No names released yet until the family is notified."

My dad walked in the house from cutting firewood to a hysterical stepmom, called my mother in Washington, and for the next hour my family didn't realize they were the lucky ones.

There are a lot of families out there who aren't as lucky as mine, and oftentimes the stories of the great things their loved ones did are never told. Mike was a great deck boss and mentor. He taught me things that to this day I still use. The one thing I'll always carry with me is the fact that he believed in me and thus made me believe in myself.

One thing that crab fishing in the Bering Sea will leave you with is the self-confidence and knowledge that no matter how rough life seems, it's really not that bad. Hunker down, weather out the storm, and come out the other end a better man. Maybe a little worse for wear, but a better man all the same.

The one thing I've learned through my thirteen years fishing is the sense of pride in knowing that your hard work is feeding the world. And after the battle of another season, it's great coming together with family and friends and enjoying the bounties of a good harvest, sitting down, eating, drinking, and celebrating another victory with those you love and care about.

A lot of these recipes are mine, my brother's, and collaborations or ideas with others. But the end result is the same. All are meant for celebrating life by coming together and breaking bread. And who better to share recipes with than those who have a passion for harvesting and preparing great seafood?

Slimy Limey Coconut Sundae

Banana Lumpia with Crème Anglaise

Grilled Peaches

Strawberries and Balsamic Tar

Banana Split with Coconut Caramel
and Kaffir Lime Maple Syrup

Cinnamon Buns

Hot Peanut Butter Fudge Topping

Peach Cobbler

Seafoam Peanut Butter Pie

I poached this recipe from a catering client. I was cooking for a lunch business party on Cinco de Mayo, and my client said she would take care of the dessert. She gave me the recipe, and I have to admit, when I saw the ingredients, I was not that impressed, but you know the saying "Don't judge a book by its cover." This dessert is simple goodness. It is the perfect ending to any spicy Mexican meal.

SLIMY LIMEY COCONUT SUNDAE

1 Scoop the ice cream into 4 bowls or cups. Sprinkle each with ¼ cup of the toasted coconut. Squeeze the juice from ½ of a lime over each serving of ice cream.

Makes 4 servings

½ gallon French vanilla or vanilla bean ice cream

1 cup toasted coconut

2 limes, halved

BRO' NOTE:

PAY ATTENTION WHEN TOASTING THE COCONUT, 'CAUSE THE COCONUT WILL TOAST VERY FAST UNDER THE BROILER BECAUSE OF ITS HIGH SUGAR CONTENT.

BRO' NOTE:
ATTENTION: NEVER FIND YOURSELF IN THE END OF THE LINE FOR THIS DESSERT. YOU MIGHT FIND AN EMPTY PLATE. I'VE SEEN IT HAPPEN . . . TO ME.

All you mainlanders are probably wondering, what in the heck is a lumpia? It's a Filipino dessert that I learned how to make working in hotels around Hawaii. You pretty much take and wrap a banana in a spring roll wrapper, and in this recipe you dip it in crème anglaise, which is the base sauce for ice cream.

BANANA LUMPIA WITH CRÈME ANGLAISE

1 To make the crème anglaise, in a medium saucepan, scald the milk and add the sugar and the vanilla bean, stirring until the sugar is melted. Remove from the heat.

2 Whisk the yolks in a metal bowl. Temper the eggs with 1/3 of the milk mixture and pour the egg mixture back into the saucepan. Heat over low heat until the créme thickens. Cool the sauce in the refrigerator.

3 To make the lumpias, cut the bananas in half. Place in a medium bowl and toss with the brown sugar, cinnamon, and rum. Marinate for 30 minutes.

4 Place 1/2 inch warm water in a large pan. Place one spring roll wrapper in the water for 10 to 15 seconds. Carefully remove and place on a dry surface.

5 Place a banana half about an inch from the edge of the spring roll wrapper, fold the edge up, the sides in, and roll. It should look like an egg roll. Seal with the beaten egg. Continue with the remaining wrappers and bananas.

6 Place the oil in a large stockpot over high heat and bring to 350°F. Carefully place the lumpias in the hot oil and deep-fry till golden brown.

7 To serve, cut on the bias, dust with confectioners' sugar, and dip in the crème anglaise.

Makes 8 servings

Créme anglaise:

4 cups milk

1 cup sugar

1 vanilla bean, split

6 egg yolks

Lumpia:

4 bananas

1 tablespoon brown sugar

1 teaspoon cinnamon

1 tablespoon dark rum

8 lumpia or spring roll wrappers

1 egg, beaten

4 cups vegetable oil, for frying

1/2 cup confectioners' sugar

GRILLED PEACHES

4 fresh, ripe peaches

nonstick cooking spray

½ cup brown sugar

1 teaspoon cinnamon

vanilla ice cream

1 Preheat the grill to medium-high.

2 Cut the peaches in half and remove the seeds. Spray with cooking spray and place facedown on the grill. Grill for 2 to 3 minutes, flip, and equally cover each peach half with brown sugar and cinnamon. Close the grill and continue cooking until the peaches are semisoft. Serve each with a scoop of vanilla ice cream.

Makes 8 servings

I was at a dinner party in Tampa, making the Reckless Red Salmon and using my friends as my guinea pigs and test subjects, when my buddy Rob, a fly-fishing guide in the Keys, busted out the balsamic reduction on ice cream . . . Unbelievable.

STRAWBERRIES AND BALSAMIC TAR

1 Put the vinegar in a saucepan and reduce by half over low heat.

2 In the meantime quarter the strawberries. Set aside.

3 Scoop the ice cream into sundae dishes or lowball glasses. Top with strawberries. Drizzle with the balsamic tar, as we call it.

Makes 4 servings

2 cups balsamic vinegar

2 pounds fresh strawberries, washed and capped

vanilla ice cream

BRO' NOTE:

STRAWBERRIES AND BALSAMIC—A GREAT COMBINATION, SO I FIGURED I WOULD THROW THEM IN THE MIX.

BANANA SPLIT WITH COCONUT CARAMEL AND KAFFIR LIME MAPLE SYRUP

1 To make the caramel sauce, place the sugar in a large, heavy saucepan and melt it over medium heat, stirring constantly with a wooden spoon. This will take 2 to 3 minutes. Continue cooking until it begins to caramelize, 3 to 5 minutes. You are looking for a golden-brown color.

2 Remove the pan from the heat and stir in the coconut milk. Return to the heat and bring the sauce to a boil. Stir in the cinnamon stick and lemongrass. Reduce the heat and simmer until the mixture is thick and rich in flavor, about 10 minutes.

3 In a small bowl dissolve the cornstarch in water and stir into the saucepan. Simmer for 1 minute until thickened. Remove from the heat and remove the cinnamon stick and lemongrass. Refrigerate until the sauce is cold.

4 To make the Kaffir lime maple syrup, place the maple syrup and the kaffir leaves in a saucepan over low heat. Bring to a boil and remove from the heat . Let stand for an hour to cool. Remove the leaves.

5 To serve, place two banana slices in each bowl or banana split boat. Top with ice cream, caramel sauce, lime syrup, nuts, and shredded coconut.

Makes 4 servings

Caramel sauce:

2/3 cup brown sugar

2 cups coconut milk

1 cinnamon stick

1 stalk lemongrass, flattened with knife

2 teaspoons cornstarch

1 tablespoon water

Kaffir lime maple syrup:

1/2 cup maple syrup

2 kaffir lime leaves

Splits:

4 bananas, split lengthwise

1 pint vanilla ice cream

1/2 cup chopped macadamia nuts

1/2 cup toasted shredded coconut

CINNAMON BUNS

Dough:

1/2 cup warm water

2 envelopes active
dry yeast

1/2 cup sugar plus 1
teaspoon sugar, divided

1/2 cup milk

1 teaspoon salt

4 tablespoons butter

2 eggs

4 1/2 cups sifted all-
purpose flour, divided

Filling:

1/2 cup (1 stick)
butter, softened

1 cup light brown sugar

1 cup raisins

1/2 cup chopped walnuts

1 tablespoon ground
cinnamon

1 To make the dough, place the warm water in a 2-cup container. Sprinkle the yeast into the water. Stir in 1 teaspoon of the sugar and let stand for 15 minutes, until the mixture begins to foam.

2 In a medium saucepan, heat the milk, the remaining sugar, salt, and butter, stirring just until the butter melts; pour into a large bowl and allow to cool slightly. Beat in the eggs with a wire whisk until well blended. Stir in the foaming yeast mixture.

3 Beat in 2 cups of the flour until smooth; stir in enough of the remaining flour to make a soft dough.

4 Turn the dough out onto a lightly floured pastry board and knead until smooth and elastic, about 5 minutes, until the dough no longer sticks to the surface.

5 Place the dough in a large, greased bowl; turn over to bring the greased side up. Cover and let rise in a warm place for 1 to 2 hours, until the mixture doubles in bulk.

6 To prepare the filling, in a small bowl combine the butter and brown sugar until well blended. Stir in the raisins, nuts, and cinnamon. Set aside.

7 Divide the dough in half; on a lightly floured pastry board, roll out the dough to a 15 x 9-inch rectangle. Spread half of the raisin and nut mixture over the dough. Roll up, jelly-roll style, starting with the short end. Cut into 9 equal slices.

8 Place each slice, cut side down, into a buttered square 8 x 8-inch baking pan. Repeat with the remaining half of the dough and filling to make a second pan of buns.

9 Cover the pans; let the rolls rise in a warm place for 45 minutes or until double in bulk.

10 Preheat the oven to 375°F.

11 Bake the rolls for 25 minutes until golden brown. Remove from the oven and invert the pans over a wire rack or wax paper. Cool and frost with your favorite icing.

PEACH COBBLER

1/2 cup (1 stick) butter

1 cup all-purpose flour

1 cup sugar

2 teaspoons baking powder

pinch of salt

3/4 cup milk

1 (32-ounce) can sliced peaches, undrained

1 Preheat the oven to 350°F.

2 Melt the butter in a 13 x 9-inch cake pan.

3 In a large bowl combine the flour, sugar, baking powder, salt, and milk. Mix well.

4 Pour the batter into the buttered pan. Pour the peaches and juice over the batter. DO NOT STIR.

5 Bake for 30 minutes.

1 In a medium saucepan over medium heat, add the peanut butter, Nestle's powder, and water. Stir and cook until the mixture is thick. Serve hot over ice cream.

HOT PEANUT BUTTER FUDGE TOPPING

1 cup peanut butter

1 cup Nestle's Quik powder

2 to 3 tablespoons water

1 In a large bowl beat the cream cheese till fluffy and add the milk and peanut butter. Beat till smooth. Stir in the lemon juice and vanilla. Fold in the whipped cream. Pour into the crust and chill for 4 hours. Refrigerate uneaten portions.

SEAFOAM PEANUT BUTTER PIE

1 (8-ounce) package cream cheese, softened

1 (14-ounce) can sweetened condensed milk

3/4 cup peanut butter

3 tablespoons lemon juice

1 teaspoon vanilla

1 cup whipped cream

1 graham cracker pie crust

RUBS, SAUCES, AND DIPS

Chipotle Lime Butter

Rub-a-Dub Rib Rub

Pineapple-Chile-Basil Glaze

Mexican Spice

BBQ Sauce

Pico de Gallo

Tartar Sauce

Cocktail Sauce

Pineapple Bruschetta

Jason's Tropical Coconut Dip

Hoisin and Bourbon Glaze

Thai Pesto

CHIPOTLE LIME BUTTER

I owe this one to my friend and restaurant owner Diane. She is the one I call when I need a fresh outlook or a different view on a dish or ingredient. I was looking for something other than your average garlic butter, and this was her suggestion. It is now a favorite, and I have used it for more than just crab.

1 Melt the butter in a small saucepan. Add the chipotle, lime juice, and cilantro. Salt to taste.

2 Serve as a sauce for crab or any shellfish.

Makes 8 servings

1 cup (2 sticks) butter

1 chipotle in adobo sauce, chopped

juice from 1 lime

1 tablespoon chopped cilantro

salt

BRO' NOTE:

THE ADOBO SAUCE IS THE SAUCE THE CHIPOTLE PEPPER IS COOKED AND CANNED IN.

RUB-A-DUB RIB RUB

1 In a small bowl add the paprika, garlic, onion, cumin, coriander, cinnamon, brown sugar, pepper, and salt. Mix well. Apply generously to ribs, chicken, or brisket.

Makes enough rub for 6 racks of ribs

1/4 cup smoked paprika

1 tablespoon
granulated garlic

1 tablespoon
granulated onion

1 tablespoon cumin

1 tablespoon coriander

2 teaspoons cinnamon

2 tablespoons brown sugar

1 tablespoon
cayenne pepper

1 tablespoon salt

PINEAPPLE-CHILE-BASIL GLAZE

1 In a small bowl add the pineapple preserves, vinegar, basil, red pepper, garlic, salt, and pepper. Whisk to combine.

Makes 8 servings

3 tablespoons pineapple preserves

2 tablespoons rice vinegar

1 teaspoon chopped basil

$1/8$ teaspoon crushed red pepper

1 clove garlic, minced

$3/4$ teaspoon salt

$3/4$ teaspoon pepper

BRO' NOTE:

THIS IS A VERY GOOD GLAZE TO BRUSH ON PAN-FRIED COD FILLETS.

MEXICAN SPICE

1 In a bowl add the cumin, coriander, chili powder, garlic, onion powder, and salt. Mix well. Use as a rub for pork butt or to season any meat for tacos or your favorite Mexican dish.

2 tablespoons cumin

1 tablespoon coriander

2 tablespoons chili powder

1 tablespoon granulated garlic

1 tablespoon onion powder

1 tablespoon salt

BBQ SAUCE

1 Preheat the olive oil in a small saucepan over medium-high heat. Add the onions, garlic, and jalapeño, and cook until the onions are translucent. Add the vinegar and mustard and cook until reduced by half. It should be very fragrant and kind of burn your eyes. Add the ketchup, coffee, soy sauce, molasses, Worcestershire sauce, honey, salt, and pepper and bring to a boil. Lower the heat and let the sauce simmer for 30 minutes. Strain and cool.

2 tablespoons olive oil

1 onion, small diced

4 cloves garlic, minced

1 jalapeño, diced

½ cup apple cider vinegar

2 tablespoons Dijon mustard

2 cups ketchup

½ cup old coffee

¼ cup soy sauce

2 tablespoons molasses

2 tablespoons Worcestershire sauce

¼ cup honey

1 tablespoon kosher salt

1 tablespoon black pepper

BRO' NOTE:

THIS GOES GREAT WITH RIBS, BRISKET, CHICKEN, OR ANY PROTEIN YOU MIGHT THROW ON THE GRILL—EVEN TOFU.

PICO DE GALLO

1 In a large bowl combine the tomatoes, onion, jalapeño, cilantro, lime juice, sugar, salt, and cumin. Place in the refrigerator for an hour to let the flavors combine. Serve with tacos, burritos, or as a condiment for Mexican night.

Makes 4 servings

BRO' NOTE:

IF YOU WANT A SMOOTHER SALSA, ADD ONE (14- TO 16-OUNCE) CAN OF CHOPPED TOMATOES AND BLEND WITH A HAND BLENDER.

4 Roma tomatoes, small diced

1/2 yellow onion, small diced

1 finely diced jalapeño

1 bunch cilantro, chopped

juice of 1 lime

1 teaspoon sugar

1 teaspoon salt

1/2 teaspoon cumin

TARTAR SAUCE

When being surrounded by the freshest seafood in the world, you probably should have a good tartar sauce recipe. This is our version that goes great with fish, shrimp, or crab.

1 Place the onion, pickles, garlic, and capers in a food processor and pulse until finely chopped. Pour the mixture into a small bowl and add the dill, Worcestershire sauce, mayonnaise, Tabasco, lemon juice, salt, and pepper. Stir to combine. Place in the refrigerator and chill for an hour to marry the flavors. Serve with your favorite seafood dish.

Makes 8 to 10 servings

¼ cup small-diced onion

4 small whole pickles

1 clove garlic

1 teaspoon capers

1 teaspoon dill

½ teaspoon Worcestershire sauce

1½ cups mayonnaise

1 dash Tabasco sauce

juice of ½ lemon

salt and pepper to taste

BRO' NOTE:

THIS GOES GREAT WITH FISH AND CHIPS AND BEATS ANYTHING OUT OF THE BOTTLE. IT CAN BE MADE A DAY AHEAD IF NEEDED.

COCKTAIL SAUCE

In our family everyone likes things a little on the spicy side. We add a little Tabasco or a favorite hot sauce to this to make it a little spicier than your average cocktail sauce—and why not throw a little vodka in it just for kicks?

1 In a small bowl combine the ketchup, horseradish, lemon juice, Tabasco, and vodka. Stir and taste for salt and pepper. Chill for an hour or overnight.

Makes 8 to 10 servings

BRO' NOTE:

You can never have too many condiments.

1 cup ketchup

1/4 cup horseradish

juice of 1 lemon

1 tablespoon Tabasco sauce

2 tablespoons vodka

salt and pepper to taste

PINEAPPLE BRUSCHETTA

Bruschetta is Italy's chips and salsa, and me living and cooking in Hawaii with an abundance of pineapple, I thought it would add a unique twist. This is a great first course to any Italian meal.

1 Brush the baguette slices with olive oil and toast under the broiler until golden brown.

2 Dice the tomatoes and onion and place in a mixing bowl. Add the garlic and the pineapple and stir to combine. Add the basil, remaining 1/4 cup olive oil, and vinegar and mix well. Taste for salt and pepper. Cover each baguette slice generously with the pineapple mix and serve.

Makes 6 servings

BRO' NOTE:

PINEAPPLE SALSA IS ALWAYS GOOD AND WORKS THE SAME WITH BRUSCHETTA.

1 baguette, sliced
at 1-inch bias

1/4 cup extra-virgin
olive oil, plus extra for
basting the baguettes

4 tomatoes

1/2 small red onion

1 clove garlic, diced

1 cup small diced pineapple

5 large basil leaves,
chiffonade or julienned

2 tablespoons
balsamic vinegar

1 teaspoon salt

1 teaspoon black pepper

JASON'S TROPICAL COCONUT DIP

1 cup shredded coconut

1 jalapeño, minced

1 bunch cilantro, chopped

juice of 1 lime

1 cup mayonnaise

½ cup sour cream

6 slices Swiss cheese, shredded

¼ cup shredded Parmesan cheese

1 In a small bowl combine the coconut, jalapeño, cilantro, lime juice, mayonnaise, sour cream, and Swiss and Parmesan cheeses. Serve with chips.

Makes 8 to 10 servings

BRO' NOTE:

THIS IS ALSO GREAT ON OVEN-BAKED FISH.

HOISIN AND BOURBON GLAZE

1 In a small bowl add the hoisin sauce, rice vinegar, bourbon, maple syrup, grated ginger, lime juice, chile paste, and garlic. Whisk to combine. Great as a glaze for grilled pork chops.

Makes 8 servings

1/3 cup hoisin sauce

2 tablespoons rice vinegar

2 tablespoons bourbon

2 tablespoons maple syrup

11/2 teaspoons fresh
grated ginger

11/2 teaspoons lime juice

1/2 teaspoon chile paste

1 clove garlic, minced

1 In a food processor, add the basil, cilantro, parsley, mint, ginger, garlic, nuts, and cheese. Pulse and slowly add the olive oil until the mixture is smooth. Serve with grilled pineapple (page 162) and halibut.

Makes 6 servings

THAI PESTO

2 ounces fresh basil

4 ounces fresh cilantro

2 ounces fresh parsley

2 ounces fresh mint

1/4 cup grated fresh ginger

2 cloves garlic

1/4 cup macadamia nuts

1/2 cup grated
Parmesan cheese

1/2 cup olive oil

ABOUT THE AUTHORS

Travis Lofland is a world traveler, adventurer, offshore powerboat racer, Bering Sea crab fisherman, and TV personality. For over 12 years he has cooked in some of the world's roughest waters and caught some of the freshest seafood on the globe. He is always on the lookout for his next big adventure.

Jason Lofland trained at Le Cordon Bleu and has managed some of the top restaurants and resort restaurants in Alaska and Hawaii. From the time he was able to see over the stove he was cooking and integrating local flavors into tantalizing dishes. His motto is "You catch it, I'll cook it."

INDEX